Loving the Alien
How to Parent Your Tween
JoAnn Schauf, MS

Loving the Alien
How to Parent Your Tween

JoAnn Schauf, MS

Tasfil Publishing LLC

To my favorite people: my children—
Carrie, Nate, Ben, and Crystal—who inspire me.

To Mrs. Diane Nelson, my ninth-grade Speech and Journalism teacher at Greenacres Junior High, who imprinted on me her love of language.

To all the parents who read this and confidently
raise phenomenal tweens.

Table of Contents

Dear Parent,

This book is for you. Inside its chapters, you'll learn how to create safety and build connection with your tween. You'll discover how to pivot your leadership style to inspire and influence your tween to thrive. You'll understand their developmental tasks and empower them to move through the process of maturing easier. And you'll accept that your parenting role is much different than it was just a year ago.

Tweens often give weird messages. From the bottom of their heart, your tween wants to be heard, valued, and respected by you. Rarely would they confess that you are the most significant person in their life, but they need your unconditional love, your presence, and rides.

I know you are not looking for tricks or hacks to "fix" your tween because you don't see them as a problem. You're all in and have the capacity to tweak your perspectives and bring out the best in your beautiful tween. I invite you to keep reading. You've found your guide.

Wishing you the best,

JoAnn

Introduction

Meet Colin and his twelve-year-old son, Aiden.

When Colin arrived home from work, he heard pounding coming from his son's bedroom. He took the stairs two at a time, wondering, curious, and concerned.

As he opened the door, he found Aiden standing atop a six-foot ladder.

Aiden smiled at him from over his shoulder. "Hey, Dad! Doesn't this look great?"

"What are you doing standing on my ladder? And with my hammer?!" Not waiting for Aiden to respond, feeling more irritated, he continued, "What are those lights doing around the ceiling? And who said you could pound nails into the wall?"

"What's the big deal, Dad? Look how cool they are!" Aiden scaled down the ladder and clicked the controller. Primary colors wrapped around the ceiling looking like they were chasing each other. "Let me show you what else it can do!"

"Stop! Just stop! No one gave you permission to use the ladder or the hammer, or to play with electricity or put lights on the walls."

Aiden clicked the controller; the lights changed to a deep blue and then faded to a lighter blue. "I'm not a baby! I'm fine. Why do you have to get so upset over nothing? It's my room!"

"What makes you think you can do whatever you want? Take them down! Now!"

"No!"

Just six months prior, Aiden had been compliant. He and his parents had seen eye to eye on most things. For any desired changes to his room, clothing, or hairstyle, he would have had a chat and sought permission from his parents. Hammering lights into his wall without either of these was unexpected, and it felt wrong and disrespectful to Colin. From Aiden's point of view, expressing himself with lights and a DIY project was a no-brainer. He wanted his room to look the way he wanted, and surely his parents would like it. He lived in his room; his parents didn't.

It's important to know that Aiden's decision was not out of rebellion or malice. It just happened. When your child becomes a tween, desperate to individuate and not even a little shy about challenging everything you once both valued, they have your attention. Not that they didn't before, but now they want to make their own decisions and not have you bossing them around. This is normal. You've done nothing wrong and neither have they. But it's new and different, and I'm here to help you.

Welcome to the Age of the Alien

Chances are you relate to Colin's situation. Aiden is not the obliging boy he once was. His actions seem unprovoked, yet problematic. Colin doesn't recognize his behavior and choices. He feels frustrated and blindsided. Perhaps you've experienced a similar situation with your tween.

Up to this point, your parenting style was from the top down, being in charge or using an authoritarian approach. It usually worked well when children grew from babies to toddlers to elementary school students. Throughout, they looked up to you as the wise and caring adult they could count on. They asked permission for things and sought your approval. You were often the center of their world. Yours was a well-defined role, and you felt comfortable.

But then, nature barged in on your child's life and had its way. **Puberty** began between the ages of nine and fourteen, setting in motion this unbidden metamorphosis required to be a card-carrying adult. Suddenly, they are someone you barely recognize, and your former parenting habits, beliefs, and approaches are ineffective. More conflicts with your adolescent than you can imagine seep in.

The challenge for you, while your child is changing, is to shift your parenting style by adopting and then mastering a new mindset.

The last thing I want to do is give tweens a bad rap! They have a massive job ahead of them dealing with physical changes and sexuality, searching for their identity, and struggling with a still-underdeveloped cerebral cortex. It's a tremendous undertaking, and it's all happening at the same time. You may recall feeling what they feel—awkward, sexually aroused, self-conscious, confident, moody, powerful, and badly wanting to stand out and fit in at the same time. And a million other emotions that change in the blink of an eye.

It's with sincere appreciation for the challenges in front of them, and you, that I write this book. Let's not view ourselves or our children as the problem but see this as a remarkable time of growth and development.

You are the one who will be their leader.

When we recall Aiden's actions, it's clear that he valued autonomy, identity, and, yes, ownership. These wholesale changes often leave you, the parent, feeling threatened, baffled, and even unsure. But your role is not to hold your child back or step back. Rather, it's to support them and understand the process they are experiencing by connecting with them on a more sophisticated level and from an intuitive perspective.

The Parental Job Description, Revised

What an adolescent needs is a *leader*.

It's life-changing when you shift your role as a parent to your child's mentor, coach, and collaborator so you can influence, empower, and inspire them. Your movement from manager and enforcer to co-partner will be so beneficial that even you will be surprised.

When you realize and adopt the mindset that you and your child are in this together, rather than on opposite teams or oppositional sides, the conflicts will be fewer and cooperation greater. Your connection will increase significantly because you'll recognize that your child's changes are a necessary part of their journey to adulthood. Their alien nature is merely a placeholder!

This book teaches you how to become such a leader. Here you will learn new tools, strategies, and insights to craft this remarkable relationship with your tween—a relationship based on love, respect, and trust. Within these pages, you will learn about and understand what your child is experiencing and discover how you can approach them easily. Not to manipulate them, but to prepare and strengthen them on their journey and to empower your new role.

The concepts in this book are designed to be implemented immediately. No matter where you are on the path of raising your tween, you're ready for the calm and confidence your new skill set brings. That tween of yours is ready, too. This book introduces the **Trio of Trials: Puberty**, the **Search for Identity**, and an **Immature Prefrontal Cortex**. Each chapter provides solutions to the problems that parents just like you face.

- How to improve communication
- How to develop collaboration
- How to empower ownership of and accountability for their lives
- How to help your tween navigate sex, love, and relationships
- How to balance privilege and responsibility
- How to inspire second chances
- How to co-parent with an ex-spouse or partner
- How to promote mental health
- How to shift parent leader practices into your daily life

Yes, that may seem like a lot, but I promise you, you've got this. I believe in you. Implementing these will make your lives easier and better. And should you see yourself, or your tween, in the stories at the start of each chapter, it is 100 percent intentional.

So, now you may be wondering how you can trust me. How can I make any promises here?

Meet the Parenting Coach

I am the founder and CEO of Your Tween and You, a professional coaching and speaking practice that connects with parents to help them learn the very skills in this book. I have a master's degree in counseling. I worked in a psychiatric hospital and then as a counselor at middle school, high school, and college levels. I now coach parents, and design and present parenting workshops and professional development training sessions.

I founded Your Tween and You because something troubling stood out during my academic tenure. Parents of tweens would come to me over and over with concerns and questions about the ubiquitous phone and its pervasive social media, easily accessible troubling content, and the tendency of their children to ghost them. Their children's grades suffered, and they didn't care about what was once vibrant and important to them. Parents had no frame of reference for preparation. And they, too, were addicted to their phones.

Combining the challenges of technology with what I call the **Trio of Trials** (**Puberty**, the **Search for Identity**, and an **Immature Prefrontal Cortex**) it became my passion and purpose to help parents find effective ways to raise their tweens well and develop their parenting leadership skills.

This book is for you as you lead and launch your tween to adulthood.

Before we get started, I want you to know I believe in you and understand the struggles you and your tween face. Find comfort knowing you have found the guide you need to thrive together. You can count on my honesty.

And finally...

It will not be enough to just read this book. You must purposefully use the strategies and skills found within these pages and tweak current habits that are counterproductive to raising and honoring your tween. You'll need to appreciate and apply the insights you discover here.

Be vulnerable and real enough to step away from giving orders and dominating your child. Step into the role of coaching and mentoring. Letting go of control may not be easy for you. Who likes to do that? No one does, but the less you try to control your child, the more you hand the reins to them.

It might sound like a lot is being demanded of you—and perhaps it is. But the motivation to grow into this kind of leader is already inside you. It's like Dorothy's ruby slippers: the power has always been inside you all along. Let's get started.

Chapter 1
When Hormones, Identity, and an Immature Brain Collide

Sometimes adolescent behavior comes out of nowhere, even when you've been a middle school counselor for as long as I have.

One morning before the first bell, I looked up to see seventh grader Luke standing in the doorway to my office.

"Hey! What's up, Luke? Are you okay?"

"I have my permission slip for you," he said cheerfully.

I waved him in. "You know your science teacher expects it, right?"

"My science teacher said I could give it to you." He looked me in the eye. I knew nothing of this.

Luke enjoyed popularity, playing basketball, and taking honors classes. Typical of a thirteen-year-old boy, his size-thirteen feet didn't match his five-foot-five frame.

"Have a seat," I offered.

Luke sat in the chair across from my desk and unzipped his overstuffed backpack. His hands barely fit into it as he attempted to locate the paper. "I think I got it." He tugged with a smile. Something small and shiny flew out with it, landing with a splat on the floor.

Shock.

Both Luke and I stared at the wrapped condom in disbelief.

Silently, I watched his face turn beet red. Drops of sweat appeared on his forehead, and his eyes fixated on the condom.

Gently, I told him I was going to pick up the condom and put it in my drawer, though I doubted that he could have heard me. I did and closed the office door.

Luke hunched forward in the chair that somehow supported the weight of his mortification. He pulled his hoodie over his head, his shoulders slumped forward, and tears streamed down his face.

My heart ached for him. Of all the things he might have anticipated today, this was not one. I understood guilt and embarrassment. I knew the intensity of his worry and anxiety was exacerbated by the adrenaline and cortisol surging through his bloodstream, pumping his heart faster and robbing him of air. No cure existed for this situation.

I had no intention of asking him for an explanation. Finally, after what seemed like a very long time, with a speck of courage, he looked up at me. "You're not going to tell my mom and dad, are you?" I could hear the anguish in his voice, the fear of disappointing and failing his parents.

A Trio of Trials: Why Adolescence Is So Challenging—and What Your Tween Needs from You

Yikes! If we look at the above scene through the lens of an adult, it makes no sense. Why would a rule-following student do something so inappropriate? Why would he take the risk of getting caught? We wonder how a thriving middle school child is bold enough to bring a condom to school. It's easy to recognize how an adolescent would dissolve into tears with guilt and dread piling on in the moment. And we wonder what he possibly could have been thinking.

When we look through the lens of an adolescent, Luke's actions fall into unsurprising patterns. The series of his decisions highlight the three main changes occurring in tweens: **Puberty** with physical/sexual development coupled with curiosity, the **Search for Identity** rooted in social and belonging requirements, and an **Immature Prefrontal Cortex** affecting cognitive processing.

Physical and sexual development promotes a normal interest and inquisitiveness about all things sex. His physical and emotional responses to the condom's presence underscore his inexperience and inability to deal with the situation and his emotions. The behavioral changes manifest in his out-of-character choice can be attributed to his identifying with and being accepted by his peers. And the intellectual changes show themselves in his ignorance of and inability to process possible negative consequences.

Nature interrupts childhood and forces children to mature—physically, socially, and intellectually. They have no choice in the matter. You, the parent, on the other hand, have a choice in how you approach and respond to your changing child. The parenting strategies that worked for your elementary school child simply don't for adolescents. As you read, you will learn how to approach, understand, and respond to grow connection and respect with your tween. It begins with comprehending the specific developmental tasks they must satisfy to be a successful adult.

There's an Elephant in the Room

Before we address the extraordinary challenges and changes your tween faces, we need to address the elephant in the room: the sense of loss you as a parent of tweens may feel.

It's normal to experience a sense of loss as you experience being relegated to the cheap seats, ignored, left out, and forgotten. As difficult as it is to accept, it's true that your role as a parent to a younger child worked well then. Adolescence is, simply put, an entirely different realm.

The child who used to chatter to you endlessly about dinosaurs, dogs, or games at recess now responds to your inquiries with one-word answers. She no longer initiates a conversation and prefers instead to shut the door to her room so she can be alone or spend hours texting her friends, scrolling on social media, and watching YouTube videos.

The child who used to jump for joy if you asked him to accompany you to the post office now rolls his eyes at the invitation. You have to call him five times before he slumps into the room to see what you want. And finding out what he is thinking is impossible.

These children used to cherish and welcome your affection; they loved spending time with you. Now all they want is to know what's for dinner or for you to give them money or a ride to an event.

Parents wonder, *What happened to my beautiful, loving child? What happened to the great relationship we used to have?* These questions are as normal as they are heartbreaking. For many parents, there is a bit of grieving, for this change is a loss.

As such, a parent may feel their identity shaken: "I spent the last decade protecting and shepherding this person who doesn't want me to do that now. Who am I now that I'm not needed? What is my role?" Some parents question themselves. "What have I done wrong? Where do I fit now that my former place in my child's life has been erased?"

On the other hand, sometimes a parent likes having more free time. They appreciate not being the master scheduler, room mother, and social coordinator.

Kindly remind yourself that it's neither your value nor values that need to change; it's learning and welcoming your new role. As well, it's accepting and recognizing that as your child undergoes a tremendous evolution, transforming from a child to an adult, they have no skills to master it. They need you.

In adjusting your parenting outlook and approach, part of the normal progression of parenting, you let go of beliefs and methods no longer useful or needed. Stepping up to this challenge requires intention and a willingness to change. Once you accept this tremendous evolution, your child's accumulation of skills, and the feelings you have about it, you won't stay anchored to the old ways.

I'm with you as you accept your tween exactly as they are in the moment, vow to become their leader, and understand their struggles. For they need you to be calm and confident while navigating this massive journey and growing a new kind of relationship with them. You will inspire, influence, and empower them and their process. So, let's begin with a look at what, exactly, is going on inside your beloved child.

Because you know that nature interrupts childhood and the **Trio of Trials** is upon your tween, let's look at them from your perspective and your child's. The more you know, the better prepared you will be to understand and support them.

> **Remember, your child is not to blame; she is not a problem, nor does she need to be fixed. Our children rely on us to step up and become their leaders. The transition may take them by surprise. They may be feeling the loss of an easier time too, or be eager to join the ranks of being a teen. It's impossible to know how your child will respond. I had a student once who so badly missed the comfort, familiarity, and ease of elementary school, she often started to get out of the car when her mom dropped off her younger sibling. In contrast, another student checked his body every night hoping for armpit or pubic hair.**
>
> **It's incumbent upon you, the parent, to construct a new relationship that aligns with your changing family dynamics and your unique tween.**

Trial #1: Puberty

You are, in a way, already an expert on the physical and sexual changes of **Puberty** because you experienced it. You know the basic facts, though you have probably forgotten how you behaved and felt (who wants to remember that time of their life?). Most likely, you behaved very similar to how your tween is acting now. If you don't believe me, ask your mother or father.

The physical and sexual changes in your tween's body impact them on the mental and emotional levels. New responses to ordinary events (seen from our point of view) include forgetfulness, emotional outbursts, flashes of anger, moodiness, and attitudes previously unseen. And you might discover, as seen in Luke's story at the beginning of this chapter, that the topic of sex comes up at the oddest times. Please keep in mind that as difficult as these behaviors are for you to respond to, they are even more distressing for your child. At this point, they have zero experience dealing with their body's weird reactions.

The Unknown

Changing can be a wonderful adventure. But it is not always glorious when the change is forced or unwanted, as some children feel when **Puberty** hits.

Nature barges in, forcing its agenda that children become adults. The changes manifest in a variety of ways. A tween may express, "I used to be the fastest runner, but now I'm one of the shortest guys in eighth grade and not fast." This is a loss of place and status. Or they may say, "I hate wearing a bra. It's so uncomfortable!" This is an irrefutable truth! On the other hand, they might say, "I'm finally taller than my mom and sister." Thanks, growth spurt.

Some changes are harder to accept than others and may result in a tween feeling unsure, powerless, or agitated. A girl's first period is a good example. Even when cognitively prepared and comfortable chatting with friends about it, this is a life-changing event. Although well-stocked with supplies, when her period arrives, she may be consumed with perplexing and unfamiliar emotions that she doesn't know how to handle—as well as the inconvenience of added trips to the bathroom and physical discomfort. Plus, she has no idea when that period will end and the next will begin. The unknown and unpredictability hang over her. This bodily interruption is incredibly intrusive to girls who used to know *exactly* how their bodies worked. It's frustrating!

Keeping up with a changing body and functions is not just for girls.

The first wet dream and being sexually aroused at school may feel exciting or alarming for a boy. Again, armed with no experience, learning to deal with them takes time. If an erection is noticed by others at school, who knows what will happen?

Then there are all these questions about bodies circling the adolescent brain:

- Why do I have hair growing there?
- Why do I stink all the time?
- Why is my hair greasy?
- What's with these pimples?
- Why me? Why now? Why did it take so long to happen?
- What am I going to look like?
- Why do I have to have a period? I'm never having children.

Additionally, a boy who has not hit **Puberty** gets called a "baldy" in the locker room. A girl who physically matures early wonders, *Why are my breasts so big? When are they going to quit growing?* Mother Nature is unpredictable.

Their unease is real in spite of you preparing them for the physical and sexual changes. It's just impossible to alleviate their worries and anticipate every question ahead of time. It's no wonder their sense of self, their confidence, and even their creativity can be affected. No wonder they are on top of the world one morning and super grouchy or argumentative the next.

They must complete the tasks necessary in the physical and sexual areas to become a card-carrying adult. They have no idea that adulting is overrated! Yet, it's impossible to alleviate their worries and anticipate every question they may have ahead of time. Please be assured this process takes time, and they have you.

Sex and Gender on the Brain

The changes that come with **Puberty** create sexual curiosity, which is new for your tween. Let's face it, we never really outgrow this curiosity, yet we learn how to manage it! Adolescents may start off ambivalent and unsure about sex, or conversely, it's the shining new toy they can't quit thinking about. It's guaranteed that questions about sexuality and gender identification will arise. Fortunately, compared to even a decade ago, parents have many more tools and clearer language to communicate with their children about these issues. As parents, we need to help them with the process and accept that self-discovery with reassurance, rather than fear or shame.

It is helpful for parents to have both a broad and a specific understanding of the sexual changes that are happening. In particular, accept that your child is turning from a nonsexual person into a fully functional sexual being, complete with sexual feelings and desires. That concept is often hard to wrap your head around.

Up until now, the adults have been the only ones in your household with sexual feelings. It has been your big and special secret. But now your adolescent is thinking about it—and maybe even doing it. It's hard to accept /imagine your child as a sexual person, but it's the reality.

Developing a healthy and open relationship with your tween, in general, is vital. Your comfort and ease in talking about all things sex will affect your conversations. Even if you are willing and accepting, your son is not going to come home and announce, "Wow, I had a hard-on during math class and couldn't concentrate." But he may say something else that gives you a clue about what's going on. We'll discuss how to handle specific issues around sex, love, and relationships in Chapter 5, but for now, just be aware that these physical-sexual changes take up an enormous amount of your child's mental and emotional energy. And get ready to have ever so many more "talks" than just one.

Trial #2: The Search for Identity

Sometimes it feels like your child is a complete stranger, pulling on a new personality and a new costume every day. Even the most level-headed tween can make dramatic switches within the course of just a couple of days, as I once witnessed.

Jenny used to drop by my office to keep me caught up on everything happening in sixth grade. She was cheerful, played the flute, and liked her tight-knit friend group. I admired how comfortable she was in her own skin, wearing a school or band T-shirt, jeans, and sneakers nearly every day—she never donned anything that stood out. Her hair hung loose, and she didn't wear makeup.

One day as I walked by the cafeteria, there was Jenny dressed in all black: black shirt, black jeans, black shoes, eye makeup, and even black lipstick. And her hair was pulled back in a tight ponytail with a black band.

That caught my attention.

The next time she stopped by, she was back in her regular clothes. "Hey, Jenny," I said. "I saw you the other day in the cafeteria, and you were dressed in all black. I almost didn't recognize you."

"Oh, yeah! Well, I met these cool girls in my science lab. They wear black, listen to music I'd never heard, and like mysterious stuff. I never noticed them before, and I guess I was curious. Plus, they were so nice. They invited me to sit with them at lunch the next day. So I dressed like them."

"Ah! That must have been the day I saw you."

"Yep! But I learned something. I wasn't interested in the things that they liked. The dark side and immortals kinda scared me, and their music wasn't fun like it is in band. You know? And black isn't my color. I'm just not a Goth girl!"

It was clear that Jenny was trying on a new look with a new group of friends. This is an example of what searching for identity can look like. After her experience, she can draw a line through one item on her list of possibilities: Goth girl.

The **Search for Identity** is a key developmental task for adolescents. It's wound around belonging—being a part of something larger than yourself with like-minded peers. Answering *Who am I? What do I stand for? What do I believe in?* To support them, you can reassure them they can become the person they are meant to be.

We need to accept that struggling with their sexual or gender identity or with whether they want to be in band or archery is normal. Or even if they really believe what their parents believe anymore.

For Jenny, dressing in black and wearing heavy, dark makeup for a day was a way to try out something new to answer one of those questions. And when she realized she didn't fit in with that group, she dropped it and moved on.

Fitting In and Standing Out

The adolescent **Search for Identity** is polarized. They are faced with fitting in with peers and finding ways to stand out at the same time. Maybe they think, *I want to be in choir. My friends are in it, and we have fun together.* But also *I have a great voice and a chance to sing solos.* In other words, they want to be an accepted member of a group but also *distinct* from the group in an acceptable and admirable way. They want to be unique.

Whether they're trying to blend in or stand out, tweens want affirmation and approval from us. And they need it because they are uncertain. Fitting in is about feeling a sense of belonging, being included, wanted, and welcomed. This, of course, matters to all of us, no matter how old we are. We all want to be acknowledged and accepted and feel that we're okay. For tweens, it's a major stepping stone to finding that pace.

When a tween can say, "I volunteer at the Corgi Rescue Center" or "I'm a Student Council officer" or "I'm a forward on the Challenge soccer team," they have labeled one role in a group that is bigger than them.

Another key component of the **Search for Identity** involves physical appearance. Each morning, in an attempt to meet the unwritten expectations of adolescence, they scrutinize their chosen outfit to determine whether their peers will accept it. In middle school, students end up dressing the same without even realizing they are doing it—they just think that's how they're supposed to dress. The next time you drop your child off or go inside your child's school, look at the unassigned uniforms!

Rejecting the Old Self

Fostering autonomy is also part of the **Search for Identity**. When your tweens say, "I want to be completely on my own. I want to make my own decisions. I don't want to be told what to do," they are signaling a deep need to figure out who they are when they stand on their own.

When our children are younger, we create a sense of family identity by doing things together: taking trips, having other families over, or rooting for the same team. We have rites and rituals, and celebrate holidays and birthdays year after year.

It's the job of adolescents to question the family assumptions they have grown up with. They may end up rejecting beliefs and practices they used to accept. They might reject their family's religious beliefs, the importance of getting good grades, or the necessity of taking a bath every day. They may decide they don't want to have a bar/bat mitzvah, they don't want to be in Scouts anymore, they want to quit piano lessons, or they have no interest in decorating the Christmas tree. Nothing remains unexamined or reassessed. It's part of the challenge of being an adolescent and becoming their own person.

When tweens reject what you believe or refuse to continue with activities they used to love, you may see those actions as oppositional. You may feel they are challenging you and the status quo. But that's not their purpose. They must differentiate themselves from their parents. They wrestle with values, determine their work ethic, accept or reject risks, identify their sexual preferences, and much more.

This search is bumpy, confusing, and vacillating. Your acceptance and understanding of the process empower your child to explore the ideas safely.

Managing Your Reaction

Wise parent leadership means holding it together—and *not* overreacting to statements like "Good grades don't matter!" or "Why do we have to go to Aunt Sally's every year for Thanksgiving?" Or to your child wearing trendy mismatched socks, or shorts when it's thirty degrees outside. There are battles that are worth fighting, but for many of these identity experiments, it is better to recognize and accept your adolescent's search. If they're interested in something dangerous, talk it through rather than issuing a hard no. You must have the grace to be patient with your evolving child. We want to support and encourage this journey of identity clarification.

When I asked my students what they think about when they are daydreaming, here's what they shared:

- What would it be like if I never learned to drive a car?
- What kind of business can I start now, so I can always be the boss and have money?
- I want to graduate from high school in four years and skip all the hoopla.
- I am not sure outdoor Christmas lights are worth the trouble.
- Why does gender matter to adults?
- Why do my parents think I need to be bossed around?
- What's the practical application of knowing prepositions?
- I'm looking for evidence of God.

They were free to say what was on their mind because I wasn't going to feel threatened by what they expressed, nor was I going to judge them, make them defend themselves, or convince them to think like me.

It's hard for us parents to step into our child's curiosity without putting in our two cents worth via anxiety, opinion, or morality. Yet creating sanctuary and psychologically safe spaces for our tweens to share their ideas, dreams, and fears colors your relationship with trust and respect. (We'll discuss the superpower of "listening to understand" in Chapter 2.)

As I mentioned earlier, Jenny joined a different group for one day, yet wholesale changes in friend groups should kindle our interest as parents. For example, instead of asking to ride bikes with friends on Saturday or go to Starbucks with her friends after school, she wants to be dropped off at a park that's in a shady area of town. You are still ultimately in charge, and you still have methods of controlling their behavior and safety. In this case, for instance, you can say, "I don't feel comfortable with that" and then not provide the ride. This language puts the concern on *you* rather than questioning your child's motives.

Perhaps the hardest part of parenting an adolescent is finding the balance between regulating your emotions and listening to understand your child. We cannot see into all areas of their lives, and the unknown is scary for us (and for them), especially what happens online and on social media, even with parental controls. So often, that phone seems to be the enemy. There is no way you can afford to make technology the opponent and nemesis. That would be a battle unworthy of you, your relationship, and your tween's journey.

Our children will mimic the example we set for self-control; there is no escaping this reality. If you yell at them (because you are not controlling the emotions swirling in your brain), you are giving them permission to yell, too. Whatever the initial problem was—whether they turned the Wi-Fi back on after you went to bed, lied about the time a party ended, or something else—it becomes twice the problem because the emotional impact derails the real problem.

Trial #3: The Prefrontal Cortex

Sometimes adolescent behavior is utterly baffling.

Seventh graders Cedrick and Jacob have been best friends since third grade. One day, they stood in the lunch line and made jokes about the tater tots. As they reached the end of the line, they eyed the seats left at their usual table. The most coveted spot was still open.

"I call window," Jacob announced.

"No way! That seat's mine." Cedrick took a deep breath of confidence.

"Nu-uh. And if you try to take it, you'll be sorry."

"Yeah, right," Cedrick scoffed.

They rushed to the table, elbowing to get in front of each other. Cedrick reached the seat first. "Told you," he laughed. But, before he reached for his milk carton, Jacob threw his tray down and punched Cedrick—hard.

What on earth? Why did that boy hit his best friend?

The short answer is the Immature Prefrontal Cortex.

The Prefrontal Cortex Explained

The **Prefrontal Cortex** is the seat of the brain's executive function; it contains the ability to plan, consider consequences, suppress urges, and discern between conflicting thoughts. This is where all decision-making happens. In the adult brain, it processes questions like these: Should I do that? Will this get me what I want? What will happen in the short term and long term? Is this safe? How will I feel about it tomorrow? What are my choices?

The problem for adolescents is that this administrative processing department develops slowly—they don't yet have the capacity for solid decision-making.

When tweens act irrationally, impulsively, or dangerously, they are not thinking things through or calculating consequences. It's not the case that they decide to ignore or discount the information; it's that their brain does not supply it. It's because they can't—at least not consistently.

On that particular day, Jacob's Prefrontal Cortex functioned poorly. He acted on impulse. He wanted that seat. His friend took that seat. So, he hit his friend. He didn't consider the consequences, weigh the value of the friendship, consider kindness, suggest taking turns, or offer it to him. Not one of these things occurred to him. His vision was myopic.

It's important for parents to understand that adolescents don't intentionally behave like weirdos. They simply don't have the brain bandwidth and decision-making ability adults do. In fact, the Prefrontal Cortex does not fully develop until a person is between twenty-one to twenty-five years old. It can be confusing: your child is as tall as you and physically grown up, but they still operate with inconsistent and ineffective executive functioning abilities. This mature-looking person is still very much a child.

However, I'm not just talking about rational decisions here. The limbic system, in particular the amygdala, which controls emotions, is growing. Tweens immediately react to emotions like fear and aggression or have an instant sexual response because the amygdala doesn't know how to best process those feelings yet. The maturation into adulthood is very much a matter of the amygdala maturing and processing emotional information, without getting stuck on an emotion, so that the information can move into the **Prefrontal Cortex** where reason and logic can be applied before deciding, before taking action. That maturation doesn't happen overnight, so adolescents operate in a muddled and perplexing environment—only they don't realize it.

Emotional Overload

Unlike body hair and broader shoulders, some of the physical changes of **Puberty** are invisible—they happen *inside* the body. So, to understand some tween behavior, we need to learn what is going on in the brain and the endocrine system, which controls hormones.

Specific hormones produced by the endocrine system deliver chemical messages that induce **Puberty**. The purpose is to become a sexual being who can reproduce. To the inexperienced tween, the accompanying feelings can be as intense as the chaos of the floor of the NYSE. The problem is an overload of emotions and the response to them. Fortunately, many tweens don't experience the roller-coaster effects, and they ease into the process. But the others do.

The amygdala, the emotional center of the brain, receives and decodes information from each event and experience as it occurs. Then, emotions are attached. This is not a cognitive process—emotions are not orchestrated by us but rather show up unbidden. The intensity is unpredictable. After that, the information is forwarded to the **Prefrontal Cortex**, the administrative center that deals with decision-making, processing, and action.

Because the emotional attachment to each event happens in the amygdala, there will be a proportionate emotional response to that information going forward.

Tweens don't have the capacity to process multiple stimuli. Sometimes, too much information comes in at once and overwhelms them. Their system gets overloaded, and they can't move the information forward. So, it gets stuck there, mixing and mingling with other emotions. They ruminate on it, mentally chewing on it like a cow chews its cud, obsessing over how unfair something is or how awful it is or how important it is to have something. Or, at the other end of the extreme, they may also be obsessing over how adorable their crush is. In either case, the stimulus—the event—rests in their limbic system.

The event or information must move from the amygdala to the **Prefrontal Cortex** to problem-solve and make decisions. And to be freed of over-emoting. However, when it gets stuck in the amygdala, when they do react to it, they don't have the bandwidth to apply logic. Hence, they are swamped with emotions that can rapidly grow in intensity. This high arousal state prevents dealing with facts. The swirling grows, and the child becomes burdened by emotional overload.

But it's not just hormones pushing behavior. It's also brain development.

The **Prefrontal Cortex** doesn't support the high-intensity emotions tweens experience. As emotions get "stuck" in their brain's emotional center, they become intense and overwhelming. To them, it feels like their emotions are on fire. When they feel something, they feel it absolutely, and not just in the moment. In the brain, the memory bank and emotional centers are just a few synapses away.

As adults, when we tell the story of when we had our first kiss, failed a class, or got a speeding ticket, we might relive the memory—re-feel those emotions—because the memory is a significant one. But we don't hold on to the emotion for long or let it color our behavior because we processed it when it happened. Still, we may cherish the memory or the lesson we learned.

I can joke and laugh now about the day I received two speeding tickets. The first ticket, in the predawn hours driving from Austin to

Dallas, completely surprised me. Anger and frustration with a spoonful of guilt were attached to the event in the amygdala. Then the emotions with the event were forwarded to my **Prefrontal Cortex**. How was I going to process this? What action would I take? I had many choices. Though I felt even more pressed for time, I decided I would be a speed-limit follower.

The rest of the drive home I was ticket-free. My freeway driving was forever changed. Lesson learned!

Later, driving in my neighborhood, the application of my newly minted "driving rules" was forgotten. Ticket number two, well deserved, was handed to me by a very polite police officer. This time the emotions in my amygdala were pure disgust and anger at myself. Pushing that forward to the **Prefrontal Cortex**, the decision was clear. The monetary punishment I would incur hit a higher note on the rule-following scale. No more speeding anywhere, ever!

For me, today, the retelling of this story is hilarious. But adolescents don't have the ability to create a new perspective.

Perspective is a challenge for tweens. For example, perhaps your child's teacher called on him in class, and he didn't know the answer. He became completely embarrassed, fearing the worst. Would his teacher yell at him or think he was dumb? Would his friends make fun of him and think was dumb? Would some bully pick on him because he's obviously dumb? Some students don't know how to move forward and cognitively process the situation. All the while, you and I know to move the fears forward and realize it's okay and even normal not to know an answer. Life happens.

We need to remember that their perception is their reality. And we must respect that and help prepare them for these situations independently from the incidents.

That evening when your child tells you the story of not knowing the answer when called upon, the exact emotions resurface just as intensely as before. You may see the incident as small, but to him, it is emotionally huge. So when you say, "Don't worry about it, honey. I'm sure you'll do better next time," he can't possibly believe you. He feels dismissed and unheard. Like you want to swipe over this really big thing! His emotions are hissing and insisting it's a *big deal*, and you're acting like he forgot to put butter on his toast. Not only does his perception differ from yours, but he's also stuck in that moment. This is when he may storm off to his room or talk back to you. Meanwhile, you have no clue as to why this insignificant thing (in your mind) is wildly upsetting to him. The emotional weight continues to burden him.

Think back to our story about Luke and the condom. If an adult thought about bringing something inappropriate to work, sirens would go off. The red lights would flash. "This is a bad idea. Don't do it!" We would see the warnings and not break the unwritten rules.

Adolescents don't have that monitoring system in place yet. They react emotionally rather than with thoughtful logic. Again, it's not their fault. It's like having your computer, phone, and iPad, but they are not charged all the time, and it's impossible to keep them charged. We have to accept that this is where they are developmentally.

They need our support and to be understood.

Supporting Your Tween's Brain Development

The scary part for parents is not knowing how much risk their child will take. Will they drink? Will they skip school, steal, or cheat? Will they try drugs? Will they have sex? Will that sex be unprotected? The truth is that adolescents act on impulse, get into accidents and arguments, and misinterpret information.

It's not my intention to give you things to worry about but rather to use the information to understand and lead them.

Remember that your child's brain—and therefore, your child—is a work in progress. As they grow and develop, you can help them think critically, process information, and be aware of possibilities and risks associated with their actions. Like all skills, practicing improves results. The value of building a strong connection with your child is that you can talk together about things they are thinking about and possible ways to respond.

For example, parents can play *What Would Happen If?* It's a family dinner table or car game. In this game, you talk through how they could handle different situations.

You can start with a safe question like "What would happen if your friend didn't bring lunch to school?" and discuss the resulting consequences (hunger, embarrassment) and solutions (lend them money, share your sandwich). Once you get the hang of it, you can make the questions harder, like "What if the kid next to you at lunch had vodka in his water bottle and offered some to you? What would you do?" or "If a friend asked if he could cheat off of you, what would you do?"

With these types of conversations, you give your tween opportunities to exercise their decision-making skills in a consequence-free environment. They get to look for solutions and weigh them. Unless asked, you listen without judgment but certainly with curiosity. It's great practice for dealing with future problems. Of course, you get a turn, too.

The Positive Parts of the Adolescent Brain

Thankfully, it's not all doom and gloom or danger. For example, tweens can be great at abstract thinking and problem-solving. They can come up with very new and different ideas.

At the same time, they easily learn new technology, play a musical instrument well in one school year, and excel in algebraic reasoning. They are eager to try new things with passion and sensitivity. When they hear of injustice—like human or animal rights violations—they respond by becoming a vegan, or joining a cause, or finding people who believe as they believe.

Another plus is the adolescent sense of humor, which develops a lot in these years. As their connection to the world becomes much wider, they find so many new things funny. They will take something they heard over here and combine it with something over there and come up with a crazy new synthesis.

Though the **Trio of Trials** presents real hurdles, your child's brain development is also something that should be celebrated. Tweenhood can be an exciting time full of wonderful growth and change!

The Trio of Trials in Action: Luke's Story

Let's return to Luke, whom we left sitting in misery in my office after a condom unexpectedly fell out of his backpack. As I, and later his parents, responded to the situation, let's see how the **Trio of Trials** affected Luke's actions. And we'll learn how his parents approached him.

With a look of growing regret, Luke waited for me to respond to his question: "You're not going to tell my parents, are you?" It wasn't hard to recognize that this was his biggest fear. He needed empathy and support, not chastisement for breaking an unwritten rule.

"I know you're worried. They will need to take the condom home."

He sobbed now, tears splashing on his clothes as he reached for tissues. I was sure that, If it were possible, he'd evaporate into the floor.

"I'm here for you, Luke." I waited patiently.

"I feel so bad!" He dropped a wad of soaked tissues into the trash and grabbed more. "So, what's going to happen to me? I can't tell my parents what I did."

"I can tell them if you'd like, Luke."

"Okay. They'll be so disappointed in me. I never get in trouble." It seemed, he knew his moral compass had failed him, and he feared losing his parents' respect.

I encouraged him to take a minute in the bathroom to get refreshed and said I'd write him a pass for second period.

With his parents in my office that afternoon, I shared the morning's events. His dad sighed. "I can't believe *Luke* would do this. He's the most level-headed and reliable of our three sons. I can only imagine how horrible he felt. He had to be so embarrassed."

"Ms. Schauf, it's almost impossible to understand." His mom shook her head, sitting in the same chair where her son had sat that morning.

"I know this is upsetting to learn."

"We're grateful you told us," his mom said. "It would have been difficult for Luke to tell us. We'll talk with him tonight."

Luke's situation provides an illustration of the Trio of

Trials in action! Puberty: interest and excitement about sex. Search for Identity: he had to fit in with the group; he couldn't show up empty-handed. Immature Prefrontal Cortex: impulsivity and poor decision-making; he didn't anticipate anything could possibly go wrong.

Later, Luke's parents shared with me about how they helped their son process what had happened.

Luke thought his parents would be at his brothers' soccer and basketball games. He expected to get home from basketball practice, eat, do his homework, and go to bed before they got home, and avoid talking to them altogether.

But the house lights shone brightly. Every step to the door filled him with increasing apprehension. His feet felt like massive cement blocks. The emotions from the morning flooded him, and the lump in his throat grew. What were his parents going to say, and what could he say?

That evening, his dad opened the door, relieved Luke of his backpack, and walked him to the couch. "We know you've had a rough day, son. Come and sit with us, please." He greeted his son with the compassion he knew he needed. And the kindness he wanted to show.

Luke's mom took his hand as he sat down next to her. His sobs increased. "We know you didn't expect this or the embarrassment. Things like this don't happen to you, Luke. The stress must have been overwhelming." Because their focus centered on understanding, not accusation or anger, Luke breathed slightly easier.

His dad brought him a glass of water and tissues, and they waited together.

"Are you able to tell us what happened? We'd like to understand."

He inhaled. "In science yesterday, we were talking about...stuff. Henry—you know Henry—dared us to bring something, um, sex-related to school today. Everyone was like, 'Yeah, let's do it.' I didn't want to be

27

the one kid who looked weak or chicken."

For sure, Luke's parents were relieved that the purpose of bringing the condom was not for having sex at school.

"So, last night I, you know, decided to bring *that*."

Recognizing his predicament and pain, Luke's mom put her hand on his arm.

"That was an impossible situation," his dad said. "You didn't want to be ostracized or ridiculed by the boys in your class. You didn't mean to disrespect—."

"I'm so sorry. I feel so stupid." Luke wiped away his tears.

"I know you are. You didn't see this coming." He patted his son's leg.

"Today in science, I watched Henry and waited for him to ask us to show what we'd brought," Luke said. "But he didn't, and neither did the other guys. I felt relieved. How could I have explained what happened in Ms. Schauf's office?"

"You wouldn't have shared that."

"I don't know how I could fall for it!"

"I know you didn't see this coming and regret it 100 percent," his mom empathized. "We love you, Luke."

In addition to listening to understand Luke, and being empathetic, his parents created a psychologically safe environment for him to tell his story. This sanctuary of safety eased his pain and allowed him to express himself without fear. They showed Luke that he was their number one concern—not what had happened, but him. In no way was their intention to make him feel worse or punish him.

As a side note, Luke's parents did not express their feelings about going to school to pick up the condom. If they were embarrassed or angry, they did not share that with Luke. Not letting their emotions bleed into the discussion was another way they kept it psychologically safe for him. Their purpose centered on supporting Luke.

Taking the condom to school was propelled by his **Immature Prefrontal Cortex, Puberty**, sexual curiosity, and the desire to belong and identify with his peers. Luke, like every adolescent, will likely intersect with one or more of the **Trio of Trials** again. Each bump becomes a learning opportunity, and for Luke and his parents, a moment of connection.

You as a parent get to accept what is happening, whatever the event is, and then invest completely in your child—especially when it's uncomfortable or unpleasant. It's not the event that needs fixing; it's your presence and approach that creates security for your child.

Key Takeaways

This tremendous metamorphosis of adolescence is second only to the first year of life in terms of growth. Remember all you did to prepare for parenthood with your newborn? Already you've upgraded your parenting skills by learning about the **Trio of Trials**.

Now that you know more about the **Trio of Trials** and the tasks your child must master, perhaps you understand their position, and the quirky things they do won't seem so far-fetched. Although it will confound both of you from time to time, adolescence is also packed with moments and memories to make and savor, and plenty of things to look back on and laugh.

I believe in you and your tremendous value in your adolescent's life. Your dedicated, intentional, and purpose-filled engagement will mean more to your child than anything else. Your parenting playbook will transform as you lead, influence, and inspire your remarkable tween.

Your Key Takeaways: Your Turn to Write

Name three things you learned.

1. _____

2. _____

3. _____

Name two awarenesses you'll embrace.

1. _____

2. _____

Name at least one thing you will apply. What will you do differently?

1. _____

☼-✶✬◝⸸☾

Now that you understand what your tween is experiencing physically, socially, cognitively, and emotionally, it's time to advance your relationship by boosting your communication skills.

Chapter 2
Communicating—Boosting Your Skills for Connecting

Stephanie scrolled through emails on her phone as she waited in the middle school carpool lane. She winced when she saw Mr. Altman's email. Her daughter, Katie, had struggled with math her entire life.

It read:

> This is to inform you that Katie's overall math grade is 66. She hasn't mastered interpreting graphs yet. I've urged her to come in for tutoring the next few mornings to help prepare her for Friday's test.

Stephanie tossed her phone onto the passenger seat. She rubbed her forehead as frustration coursed through her. Why did Katie, who excelled at so many things, have to have this struggle? Would she be able to even pass seventh-grade math?

Katie swung open the passenger door. "I cannot *wait* to get some new leggings!" she exclaimed as she moved her mother's phone to the center console.

Right. They were supposed to go to the mall. Distracted by the email, Stephanie had forgotten. She pulled out of the school's parking lot with a sigh. What were they going to do?

Meanwhile, Katie didn't seem to have a care in the world. "Wanna get matching polish with me when we get our pedis? I was thinking bright orange."

"Sure." All the way to the mall, then inside Katie's favorite store, Stephanie was only partially listening as Katie chirped on about her day. All Stephanie wanted to do was discuss the math grade and what Katie's plan was for the test. But she knew she should wait until they got home.

Katie surprised her. "We started a really cool project in math today," she said as she held up a pair of leggings with four pockets.

Stephanie raised an eyebrow. "Oh?"

"It's about the stock market. We downloaded this app and invested a thousand dollars in fake money into whatever six stocks we wanted, except social media. We get to watch and see what they do. I bought Kellogg's, cuz I love Pop-Tarts and Pringles. We can buy and sell as much as we want. I might get—"

"It sounds a little complicated," Stephanie interrupted.

"It's a lot better than figuring out fractions and graphs. That stuff is so *boring*." Katie rolled her eyes.

Before she could stop herself, Stephanie burst out, "Those are really important concepts, Katie."

Katie shrugged and picked up another style. "I'm going to be a stockbroker when I grow up. I'm going to invest my money and your money and lots of people's and make us all rich. Knowing fractions or graphs isn't required."

"If you don't grasp those things by Friday, you're going to fail math, again," Stephanie snapped. "You won't even make it out of seventh grade, never mind become a stockbroker."

Katie stared at her. "Mom," she eventually said, "I'm going to tutoring all week. What else can I do?"

"You can start being more realistic! You've never understood math.

Now suddenly you think you're going to go into finance?" Stephanie couldn't quite believe what she had just heard herself say. But letting out the worries was such a relief. It felt as if she'd been holding her breath, worrying as her daughter dreamed her life away.

Katie half turned away and slowly looked through the pants. "You think I'm stupid," she accused her mom. "Don't you?"

A lead weight landed in Stephanie's stomach. "That's not what I said—"

"You don't believe in me at all. You don't care about anything except me doing exactly what you say." Katie flung a pair of leggings onto a nearby table. "I don't want anything. Let's just go."

"You're twisting my words." Stephanie picked up the pair Katie discarded and held them out to her. "Now, we came to get these, and that's what we're going to do." But Katie ran out of the store.

Stephanie caught up with her at the mall's entrance. "You're being unreasonable."

"Great!" Katie shouted. "First I'm stupid, and now I'm unreasonable."

"Hush!" Stephanie admonished. "I never said you were stupid. All I said was—"

"Just stop, okay? I'll never be smart enough for you. I'm a big failure! Just leave me alone. I'll call Dad, and he can pick me up." Katie stormed back inside the mall, into the crowd. Stephanie watched her go, immobilized by the explosion of emotions spewed at her.

Not for the first time when trying to communicate with Katie, Stephanie felt she'd just fallen down a rabbit hole. Why did that keep happening?

Effective Communication

You can imagine the emotional turmoil Stephanie and Katie were experiencing. In fact, you've probably been there yourself.

By the time Stephanie recognized how upset her daughter was, it was too late. Angry and upset by the math teacher's email, she let her negative emotions hijack what should have been a fun afternoon together. She created a disaster because she let her emotions drive her. Stephanie had a choice; she could have simply waited to talk about the math problem.

Because of their still-developing **Prefrontal Cortex**, adolescents are not yet able to look beyond themselves; their perception is their reality. It's what's in front of them and what they are feeling in the moment. In addition, as we discussed in the previous chapter, adolescents often experience exaggerated emotions. When Stephanie criticized Katie, her daughter felt betrayed, unsupported, and dishonored. Katie didn't have the capacity to look at it any other way. The extreme frustration, disappointment, and anger were all real.

Parents have told me they felt instant remorse when they let their emotions get out of control. Without thought, insulting and hurtful words fly out of their mouths. And it's never intentional.

Effective communication, on the other end of the spectrum, begins with listening to understand. It also requires recognizing and regulating emotions, empathizing, and asking questions that will elicit more information from your tween rather than shutting down the conversation.

This chapter is about how to develop these necessary communication skills so you and your tween can connect instead of clash.

Every parent has the ability to control the conversation with their tween. That statement may seem ridiculous given tweens' instant response times. Yet it is true. As the leader in the relationship, parents direct the dialogue just as a pilot maneuvers a plane. The tone, the content, and the overall trajectory of the exchange are under a parent's purview. Accepting this leadership skill is necessary. Please realize how much power you have every time you communicate with your child.

Skill 1: Listen to Understand

Listening to understand is not as easy as it sounds.

When we listen to understand, we put everything else aside. We stop what we are doing, look at the person speaking, and give them our full attention. We are actively curious and ready to learn something we don't know. We want our child to feel heard and know that we are present for them.

Listening to understand is difficult because people are busy and distracted. Our phones, in particular, create the temptation to give less than our full attention to our child. Often, we end up missing the entirety of their story. Our ears perk up when we hear words of concern. Then we turn our attention to them and ask for specifics. But your child wants you to hear the entire thing.

For instance, when your tween comes home and talks about their day, you might be scrolling through texts and saying "uh-huh," until you hear the phrase "and then the assistant principal," at which point your attention flies over to your child, and you say, "What? What happened? Are you okay or in trouble?"

If instead you listen to understand, you'll put down your phone when your tween wants to share something with you. And you will hear everything they say. And learn from their body language. And understand what's on their mind and heart. And not overreact to high-anxiety words. And be grateful that your child wants to chat with you.

When they explain that they were sitting at lunch with two students who had skipped class, and the assistant principal accused your child of skipping too, you can respond with empathy and curiosity. "Gosh, you weren't expecting that" or "That must have felt weird." As they continue on and tell you that the assistant principal eventually apologized, you can respond, "You must have felt relieved. You've never gone through anything like this before."

Tweens tell you the stories of their day because you express interest, curiosity, and empathy. They feel safe sharing because you don't gasp, pepper them with questions, launch into a lecture, interrupt, or let your emotions bleed into the conversation. They feel heard and respected.

You can become a better listener by learning how to create conversations of substantial value. Eventually, your preparation will become a habit, so that you listen effectively even when your child springs a major talk on you in the middle of the cereal aisle or on the drive home from a fencing lesson.

35

Here are three steps to follow.

1. **Shift your purpose**: Your purpose when conversing is not to *be understood* but to *understand*. You want to gain information, not give it. Note that this shift is not just for listening to your child—you can use it with your boss, your spouse, and everyone else in your life. Your goal is to comprehend what is going on in the speaker's world. Visualizing who's holding the microphone is helpful. If you are talking, you are not learning or listening.

2. **Be quiet and be present**: Give your full presence to the speaker. Get rid of distractions—especially your devices and internal monologue. Your body language should indicate you are focused on the speaker. Make eye contact, nod to show understanding, face the speaker, and breathe.

3. **Honor the person speaking**: Realize that when you are listening, you are prioritizing your child in a sacred space and time. This builds trust and respect. Do not interrupt, chime in with your similar experience, talk over them, correct them, or give advice. They want to share their world with you.

One more thing: less is more. You don't need to do a lot of talking when you are listening!

Skill 2: Regulate Your Emotions

In Katie's story, Stephanie let her anxiety and frustration dictate how she communicated with her daughter. Although we talk a lot about how tweens must learn to cope with overwhelming feelings, it is equally important for parents to regulate their emotions as they interact with their tweens.

Emotional Literacy

Before we talk about emotional regulation, we need to talk about the elements of emotional literacy: it is the ability to identify and understand your feelings and the feelings of the person you're talking to, and the ability to manage your emotions.

Emotional literacy requires observing, monitoring, and reading emotions. Emotions reveal themselves in words and by observable clues. These include mood, attitude, body language, tone of voice, eye contact, facial expressions, tears, laughter, and smiling. In addition, physical signs—pushed by rising adrenaline levels such as a red face, sweating, being unable to catch one's breath, and shaking—provide input for emotional identification. Learning to decode these outward signs will provide you with a wealth of important information about your child's emotional status and yours.

It's a lot of work to identify and understand someone else's emotions, let alone your own. Most of us didn't get past Emotions 101, so getting a boost now will serve you well. To be emotionally literate, you must be self-aware and introspective about your emotions so you can name them. Conversely, naming your child's emotions is necessary as well. You must also remain calm. It takes practice, practice that is well worth it because communicating on this level builds connection and trust. And you want this.

Remember, emotions are bits of information that tell us more about what is going on. No emotion is ever right or wrong. Nor should it be downplayed, fixed, or ignored.

It is also important to recognize that a parent and child will likely have different emotions about the same situation. To get a feel for how this plays out, consider these examples:

Example 1:

Fabián is at the end-of-the-year award ceremony. He's excited because his daughter Alicia is a brilliant science student, and he is expecting her to get the science award. He has even invited Abuela and Tía Rosa to come to the ceremony. But then Alicia doesn't get the award.

- How does Fabián, the dad, feel? Embarrassed? Okay? Worried? Self-conscious? Judged? Something else?
- How does Alicia feel? Indifferent? Content? Disappointed? Embarrassed? Something else?

Example 2:

Thea's son Graham texts her to say that he left his portion of his group project at home. The group is supposed to present today. Neither Thea nor her spouse can fetch the work and bring it to school.

- How does Thea feel? Regretful? Annoyed? Guilty? Not surprised? Something else?
- How does Graham feel? Disappointed? Remorseful? Anxious? Angry? Accepting? Something else?

Example 3:

Keisha's child Avery has been invited to their best friend's birthday party this weekend. However, Avery is not passing English, and they agreed at the beginning of the school year that if they were not passing a class, they would spend the next weekend working to improve their grade. That includes no social or fun things. Avery asks Keisha if they can go to the party anyway.

- How does Keisha feel? Resolute? Sad? Conflicted? Something else?
- How does Avery feel? Hopeful? Resentful? Scared? Something else?

The point of this exercise is to improve your awareness that many different emotional responses are possible to the same situation, and that you as the parent may not feel the same way as your child. Remember, no matter what the feeling is, it is okay.

Maybe Alicia is relieved she doesn't have to walk up on a stage in front of all those people.

Maybe Graham is furious that his mom, who always bails him out, has picked this time to say "no."

Maybe Keisha, who is usually very strict, is surprised to find herself feeling indulgent toward her child.

Remember that you cannot know how your child will feel in any given situation. Instead, observe, listen, be curious, and keep an open mind. These efforts will go a long way in helping you understand their emotional experience.

Be mindful that there is a wide range of emotions beyond the basics of glad, happy, sad, and mad. You can improve your awareness of the emotional world around you by expanding your emotional vocabulary. For an Emotions Chart, see https://www.yourtweenandyou.com/emotions/. Practice observing yourself and others around you and naming the emotions you and they are feeling.

Emotional Literacy Meets Emotional Regulation

Emotional regulation is not about controlling your emotions but controlling your *reactions* to your emotions. The first part is literacy, as you learned above. The second is making a choice about how you will respond. It will make a tremendous difference in every conversation you have if you keep your negative emotions out of the conversation.

Perhaps you're triggered by a word you are sensitive to, or your child makes the same mistake again. Automatically you feel infuriated, incensed, irate. It is okay to feel exactly what you are feeling and to accept it. Remember, emotions show up unbidden, packed with bits of information, and are neither right nor wrong. What can be right or wrong is how we choose to respond.

> **Being triggered is exactly the moment where emotional regulation becomes an option. Taking a moment, a pause, to figure out your feelings and still hold it together.**

We are mistaken if we believe lashing out at a child, losing our temper, or corporal punishment will make it better, keep it from happening again, or solve the problem at all. We know it doesn't work that way. In fact, a parent's emotional outbursts add an additional layer to conflicts, something made evident in a recent argument between Tom and his daughter Margaret.

Tom was aggravated at Margaret for having her phone in her room at night. It was a two-part issue because her phone is supposed to charge after 9:00 p.m. in the kitchen, and she lied about it. His anger was palpable; he felt disappointed and exasperated. This lie was one in a long line of mistruths. He blew up, shaking his finger at her. "How many times have you lied to me? I'm sick of you lying! You know better! Where is your honesty and integrity? I raised you better than this. You've got to stop!"

His reaction upset Margaret. She was aware that he was out of control and livid. She wondered when he would stop ranting and raving. Wondered what she could do to get him to calm down. She worried about being called a liar and what kind of harsh punishment was about to come her way. And she had the fight, flight, or freeze urge to manage.

Her emotions ranged from fear, regret, shame, and embarrassment to anxiety and distress. These are understandable and impossible for Margaret to unpack by herself in the heat of the moment.

Her dad's lack of emotional regulation escalated the conflict. It became all about his emotions, rather than him focusing and working through Margaret's issues, which needed attention. It's as frightening as it is disturbing to children when their parents have what looks and sounds like an adult temper tantrum.

When you choose to process your emotions, things look differently: *I'm angry, and that's okay. I don't need to do anything about it right now because it's more important to give my tween what she needs. I feel the pain of disappointment building in me, and I will keep that to myself and deal with it after I help my child with this issue.*

The power of regulating your emotions is that whatever the conversation is about, you will stay on topic and not get emotionally wound up. Your emotions have no place in listening for understanding. As the leaders, parents are responsible for maintaining emotional control no matter what they are feeling or what their child has done or failed to do.

Practicing Emotional Regulation

Sometimes, like Stephanie reading the teacher's email, and Tom getting angry about his daughter lying, you are not ready to regulate your emotions. You know what you are feeling and how you *should* respond. It may take a moment or more to get yourself together, and that is okay. The important thing is that you create a neutral mental space where you come to terms with your emotions and your *response*. When you feel you are losing it, or will soon, it's important to ask your child for a short pause—a time-out.

To determine if you need to pause, ask yourself these questions:

- Am I calm?
- Am I able to listen to understand?
- Am I able to monitor what I say?
- Am I able to respect my child and myself?
- Am I able to set my emotions aside for now?

If you answer "no" to any of them, you need to take a break. It's perfectly acceptable to say you need some time to yourself to think about it and to suggest revisiting the issue in five minutes/at home/over dinner.

Use the time to assess your emotions, silence your inner chatter, remember your purpose, and focus on a heart-centered outcome, not a punitive one. Taking time to pause provides a model for your tweens to emulate. Encourage them to use it, too, to help develop their own skills for emotional regulation.

Emotional regulation can be practiced at any time, not just when your tween has told you they dented your car with a slapshot, or they spilled the beans about their mom's surprise birthday party. In fact, a great way to practice it is to do so when the risks are low. For instance, while on a work call, you recognize your anxiety: your heart is racing, and your mind wanders as you search your computer but can't find a file that someone needs. Armed with this awareness, you purposefully regulate your emotions by telling the person on the phone you need a few minutes and will get back to her. You are taking that moment, creating a pause to accept your antsy and worried emotions. You remind yourself to breathe, stay calm, and reassure yourself that your emotions are normal and okay. We all need self-led pep talks.

Of course, regulating your emotions is not easy. There's no pill to take. And it's not a plug-and-play operation at the beginning. Give yourself the gift of time and start by focusing on your *why*—you want to regulate yourself to keep yourself in control and show the other respect and kindness.

Skill 3: Respond with Empathy

Empathy rises to the top of the communication pyramid. It's the capacity to observe the other without judgment, use emotional literacy, and then respond to the person about their emotions. Empathy creates an emotional connection between people because it builds trust and respect.

We've all been in situations where our kid comes to us with what we immediately see as a problem that needs solving. We often go into problem-solving mode when what they actually need is to be emotionally understood in that specific time and place. See if this scenario sounds familiar:

Jadyn trudges into his mom's office and sticks a piece of paper in front of her. "Look!" he says. "I studied so hard for that science test, but I only got a 62! The teacher had all these problems that we didn't review, so I didn't know it was going to be on there."

Taking the paper and seeing the low grade in red at the top, his mom jumps into save-the-day mode. "You need to ask the teacher if you can retake the test," she says. "Start studying this afternoon, and then talk to him tomorrow before school. Better yet, email him now. I know he'll make an exception for you!"

Jadyn rolls his eyes and snatches the paper back. "You're not even listening to me! Why can't you ever understand?" He stomps out of the room, leaving his mom baffled and unable to get back to her own work.

Now consider how this situation plays out when the parent responds with empathy instead of trying to immediately solve the problem:

Jadyn trudges into his mom's office and sticks a piece of paper in front of her face. "Look!" he says. "I studied so hard for that science test, but I only got a 62! The teacher had all this stuff on there that we didn't review, so I didn't know it was going to be on there."

His mom takes the paper and sees the low grade in red at the top. She hands it back to Jadyn and, looking at him, says, "That's not what you were expecting to get. You must be really frustrated."

Jadyn wads the paper into a ball and throws it on the floor. "I'm so mad at my teacher. He's so unfair!"

His mom's empathetic response gives Jadyn room to describe his emotions and makes him feel understood. His initial outburst gives only the first layer of his feelings, but after she empathizes, his mom can see the next layer.

And there are multiple possibilities for what that second layer holds. Here is one more way the conversation could go:

Jadyn trudges into his mom's office and sticks a piece of paper in front of her face. "Look!" he says. "I studied so hard for that science test, but I only got a 62! The teacher had all this stuff on there that we didn't review, so I didn't know it was going to be on there."

His mom takes the paper and sees the low grade in red at the top. She hands it back to Jadyn and, looking at him, says, "Wow, that's not what you were expecting to get. I understand your frustration."

Jadyn collapses into the chair by his mom's desk and buries his face in his hands. "I'm such an idiot. I hate myself."

These feelings are very different from the anger in the second example and require a different approach from the parent. But because she has responded with empathy, Jadyn's mom will be able to guide him through his emotions.

Empathy means mirroring tweens' emotions so they feel understood. If your tween says, "I'm so annoyed with the teacher," and you respond with, "It's aggravating, huh?" you signal that you understand him. You will not exacerbate his annoyance by stating his emotions. What happens is that he feels cared about and that you have his back.

Empathetically naming your child's emotion will not make the emotion more intense.

To respond with empathy, look for your child's emotion and then name it in your response, such as "I can see you are frustrated" or "I can tell you are uncomfortable." Your emotional literacy skills will help you here, as will these empathetic responses:

- I don't blame you for feeling _____.
- You weren't expecting that.
- This must have been _____ for you.
- For even more helpful examples, check www.yourtweenandyou.com/empathy-statements

If you are not sure how your child is feeling, ask for clarification. For example, say, "I'm not sure if you are embarrassed or angry. I want to understand how you're feeling. Are you feeling rejected or resentful?" Asking for illumination helps tweens sort out their feelings and learn to recognize their own emotions. It also helps parents to understand those emotions.

When we seek to be empathetic, emotional literacy and regulation support it. Yet our first inclination is not always to be empathetic. Consider this example where a tween has made a bad decision that impacts more than just herself:

Amanda is holding her phone, frowning at her mom, Elisa, who has just walked in to remind her to set the table. "You know those earrings Grandma gave me for Hannukah that are family heirlooms?" Amanda pauses. "I loaned them to Isabel last week, and she just told me she lost one!"

What Elisa may be thinking is: *Do you know what those earrings mean to your grandmother? Why in the world would you loan them to anyone? Where is your sense of respect for our family? What were you thinking? You didn't get permission!*

But her response centers on Amanda's feelings, not her own. What Elisa says after a moment to get her emotions under control is: "That had to be hard to hear. I can tell you feel sad."

Elisa may also feel a strong urge to problem-solve and yell something like "Call Isabel right now and demand that she finds it!" Instead, she chooses to respond with empathy so that Amanda can further explain how she feels. Understanding Amanda's emotions will send this conversation into a more positive direction.

Amanda is free to say, "I'm so sorry. I didn't think anything like this would happen. Isabel has been my best friend forever, and I trusted her. I don't know what to do."

This is the kind of conversation you want to have—to learn about your child's experience, to hear the story, details, and her feelings. Ultimately, it is Elisa's empathy without judgment that gives Amanda the psychological safety to share.

Your empathy lets your child know that their emotions are okay and that they feel understood and accepted.

Skill 4: Ask Open-Ended Questions

It's important that parents learn how to ask open-ended questions instead of questions that only require one-word answers like "yes" or "no" and the canned response of "fine." With open-ended questions, we invite ourselves into the tween's world and give them the opportunity to talk.

A common parent-tween routine is the following: it results in getting zero information.

Will comes into the kitchen where his dad, Oscar, is making dinner. He kicks off his sneakers and takes a beverage from the fridge.

"How was school?" Oscar asks as he stirs his sauce.

"Fine," Will says.

"Are you hungry?"

"Nope."

"Do you have any homework?"

"Yeah."

Will is already on his way out when he answers. He disappears around the corner and up the stairs as his dad keeps stirring, wondering if he will ever know anything about his son's life again.

But what if Oscar asked open-ended questions instead?

Will comes into the kitchen where his dad, Oscar, is making dinner. He kicks off his sneakers and takes a beverage from the fridge.

Oscar stops stirring his sauce and looks at his son. "Hey, you had sectional tryouts today. Walk me through how it went."

Will is about to head upstairs but turns around and goes to the counter. "I was supposed to play the second movement, right? But I started playing the first by accident! I just stopped and started laughing because what else could I do?"

"I like your creative and funny response," Oscar says.

Will grins. "They laughed too! And then I got to start over."

This approach opens the conversation door. It asks for a story. Using phrases like "Tell me about" and "I'm wondering" provides an opportunity for your adolescents to talk about what *they* want to talk about. Instead of simply exchanging data or discussing logistics—What time is the game? Which gym is it in? When is the test? Are you hungry?—you get stories about their lives.

And it's those stories that you really want to hear.

Open-ended questions are not just about feelings. They are also about thinking and working through choices. They are thought-provoking and can help with problem-solving.

Here are some examples:

- If you could redo it, what would you do differently?
- Tell me three things about...
- What pros and cons are you considering?
- How are you thinking about handling that?
- What will you say to your friend?
- Help me understand...
- What else did you notice?

Again, there are more examples on my website, at https://www.yourtweenandyou.com/examples-of-open-ended-questions-statements/.

Effective Communication in Action: Katie's Story

Let's think back now to Stephanie and Katie's argument in the mall. If Stephanie had a time machine, she could go back and redo their interaction using all the communication skills from above.

Let's go back to the moment when things went wrong:

Katie surprised her. "We started a really cool project in math today," she said as she held up a pair of leggings.

Stephanie raised an eyebrow. "Oh?" She realized she had a good chance to learn more about the very class she's worried about. She'd relegated her intense feelings of dread and disappointment about her daughter's math struggles for later that evening. She turned to her daughter to give her all of her attention and chose an open-ended question. "Tell me about it."

"It's a stock market game. We downloaded this app and invested a thousand dollars in fake money into whatever six stocks we wanted. Now we get to watch and see what they do. We can sell or buy more if they split, and diversify our portfolio. The idea is to see who can make the most money."

Stephanie heard the excitement in Katie's voice. "I can tell you're excited about it," she said, wanting Katie to know she could recognize her emotion. "It sounds fun. What else did you learn?"

"I learned that anyone could invest. It's not just for certain people. And I thought really carefully about what stocks I picked. Apple was the first, cuz you know I'm in love with my phone!" As Katie described her other choices, Stephanie loved seeing the concentration on her daughter's face and was amazed at the careful logic she used.

"I love hearing about all this and seeing how confident you are," Stephanie said. She noticed her own anxiety settling as she focused on Katie's feelings rather than her own worries. They soon settled on two pairs of leggings and headed to the nail salon, with Katie talking about the stock market project all the while.

"You're really good at explaining this," Stephanie said as they walked along, happy to find a way to affirm her daughter. "Maybe when you do your homework tonight, you can show me how it works."

"Sure! I really like doing this kind of stuff in math class instead of figuring out fractions and graphs. That stuff is so boring."

"That makes sense." Stephanie nodded. "I think lots of people like *using* math more than they like learning the concepts."

"But I mean, now I kind of get why I have to learn those things. By the way, I need to get to school early the rest of the week so I can get tutored before my test. I'm nervous I won't do well. What if I'm just stupid at math?"

"Math is hard, but I believe in you," Stephanie said. She was tempted to continue but stopped herself from trying to solve the problem, even though she was eager to do so.

"The teacher says my homework is always good, so maybe it's a test-taking thing. I really don't know." She picked up a bottle of orange nail polish on a stand at the front of the salon. "Oh! I totally forgot that this stock market project will raise my grade, too!"

"You like that!" Stephanie smiled, and she meant it. It wasn't just about the grade, either. It was that she didn't let her emotions ruin a great conversation—and a great afternoon—with her daughter.

Key Takeaways

If only we all had a time machine!

Communication between parents and children in the tween years is vitally important yet often excruciating. Parents must take the lead and model their values and beliefs in the way they speak to and listen to their children.

By listening to understand, parents can make their children feel valued and heard. By regulating their emotions, they can leave room for tweens to express their own. Responding with empathy helps tweens feel safe and understood. Asking open-ended questions demonstrates to a tween that their experiences are important. Plus, we get to hear the stories that make up their lives.

In addition, building these communication and leadership skills is calming for you as a parent. It gives you confidence. When you know emotions happen and that they are real, you can accept them and process them. It's that calm and confidence that we're looking for in handling the emotional side of life.

Your Key Takeaways: Your Turn to Write

Name three things you learned.

1. _____

2. _____

3. _____

Name two awarenesses you'll embrace.

1. _____

2. _____

Name at least one thing you will apply. What will you do differently?

1. _____

Now that you have developed your communication skills, you are ready to work on strengthening your collaboration skills as you and your tween solve problems together.

Chapter 3
Collaborating—a.k.a. the Disappearing Conflict Tool

S am, it's 9:00," Greg announced as he passed the kitchen on his way to the den. "Go to bed."

Sam didn't budge. With his earbuds in, he continued playing a video game on his iPad.

"Sam!" Greg said louder from the den where he settled in to relax with his wife, Carrie. "It's 9:15! I already told you to get to bed. Move. Now."

No response from Sam.

At 9:30, Greg entered the kitchen. "Sam, get to bed. I've told you twice. You're a half hour late! Turn off that iPad."

Sam pulled an earbud out. "Dad, I gotta finish this game," he said without looking up. "I'm winning for the first time."

"Turn it off now, or I'll take it."

"Hold on, Dad!"

"Give me the iPad! I am tired of you pulling this every night!"

"No! I still need to submit my math homework!" Sam yelled.

"You've had all night to do that. You are not being responsible. Give it to me NOW." Greg's face grew red.

"You don't even care if I fail math and can't play basketball!" Sam fired back.

"You should have thought about that earlier. Give me the iPad! And your phone, too. And you can forget about going to Matt's party this weekend." Yelling, Greg grabbed both devices.

"I hate you!"

"Don't you dare talk to me that way! You're grounded!" Greg shouted as Sam ran out of the room.

Sound familiar?

We've all been there. Frustrated and exhausted by the same conflict. Angry that the verbal exchange spirals into disrespect, emotional outbursts, and punishment. It's a tailspin of losing dignity and respect both ways.

In times like these, it's easy to believe that our child is the problem. After all, he's the one who's not obeying the rules. His choices ignite the fight. If only he would do as he was told, this wouldn't happen. Parents' fingers point to the child as the obvious initiator.

From Sam's point of view, however, his dad is the problem. Sam likely thinks: *Why can't he chillax and see how important this game is? And why does he have to yell and take everything away? This bedtime crap sucks. It doesn't even matter!*

The truth is that Greg's demands, threats, and yelling exacerbate the problem just as much as Sam's refusal to cooperate. There's plenty of blame to go around. Unfortunately, it's all too tempting to let yourself off the hook by embracing the idea that your child's poor behavior justifies you losing your temper or yelling. You feel angry and frustrated, and I don't blame you. Yet there is never sufficient reason to lose your self-respect or fail to respect your child. You are the leader. You set the tone for connection and problem-solving.

You can see how the communication tools from Chapter 2 could be applied to improve this interaction. This chapter builds on that by introducing a problem-solving strategy: collaboration.

When Carrie and Greg came into my school counseling office to discuss their ongoing conflict with Sam, the deep lines in their foreheads signaled their distress.

I began by telling them how much I appreciated Sam's contributions at school: his commitment to a service club devoted to students with special needs, and being chosen captain of the cross-country team by his peers. Sam was not a kid who struggled academically or socially. What I often encountered with parents was a disconnect between the behavior we see at school and what parents experience at home.

When I asked them what was going on with Sam at home, the floodgates opened, and the story of their bedtime battles poured out. When he was done recounting their latest argument, Greg sat back in his chair and let out a huge sigh. "I just don't know what to do. This happens every night, and it's not just about bedtime. Every single thing turns into a power struggle."

"I'm more than disappointed. What happened to our sweet family?" Carrie lamented.

This power struggle mirrors what many parents of tweens encounter. I could see that Carrie and Greg were ripe to rise, to learn a fresh approach to solving the bedtime issue. They were motivated because they'd lost the closeness they once shared with their son.

You can do this, too. And I hope you will, for it has proven its weight in gold.

The Interpersonal Magic of Collaboration

One of the most challenging aspects of parenting a tween is learning how to step back from the role of manager, supervisor, and superior and into the role of mentor, coach, and collaborator. You've spent a decade taking care of every need, from feeding and bathing to scheduling and educating. But now your child, a tween, no longer wants to be bossed around or controlled. This desire for independence and autonomy is a developmental marker. In order to meet it, you, the parent, need to make a profound shift in how you approach your child.

First, understand that your child is not the one that needs to be fixed—and neither are you. Throw out the blame game altogether. When your child realizes that you don't see them as the problem, they'll no longer see you as the problem. This frees you to work together on the *actual* problem, whether it's bedtime, screen time, or schoolwork.

Conflict doesn't have to be your family's kryptonite. As a leader, you have the power to break the bad habit of yelling and disrespect and instead embrace another path toward problem-solving: welcome conflicts as opportunities to learn from each other and work as a team.

Collaboration won't make conflicts disappear, but it will make solving them much more feasible by giving you, the parent-leader, a playbook to implement. But first, let's review what's going on in your child's brain when they act like Sam did when he decided to play on the iPad instead of doing his math homework before bed.

The Prefrontal Cortex: A Work in Progress

Puberty is confusing for a tween, and also a confounding time for parents. Suddenly you're looking at a young man with a deepening voice who's as tall as you are. Or maybe your daughter is having her period or comes home agog about a boy in class. They may appear mature on the surface, but as mentioned in Chapter 1, their immature brains are unable to function like a fully mature adult brain. Sometimes tweens' decisions are well thought through, and at other times they surprise you with thoughtless, risky, or immature choices. And it's completely unpredictable!

Remember that this is not their fault. Your child isn't trying to be bad or weird or out of control on purpose. They are doing the best they can with what they've got. Middle schoolers lack the capacity to weigh the consequences of their choices. This executive functioning skill requires a mature Prefrontal Cortex. To see how this works—or more precisely, how the Prefrontal Cortex *fails* to work—let's consider a seventh grader who loves and is jealous of her friend's lipstick. Without giving thought to the consequences, she takes it from her friend's purse.

Now, did our seventh grader mean to steal something? No. She focused on the lipstick: how pretty that color would be on her, and how you might even compliment her on it. She was thinking about the immediate gratification, not the consequences. She *wasn't* thinking about the fallout with her friend or ending up in the assistant principal's office. She also wasn't thinking about other ways to solve her problem, like using her allowance to buy her own lipstick. Her immature executive functioning caused the risk-taking behavior and poor decision-making.

That Prefrontal Cortex won't fully mature until around age twenty-four. That's a lot of years for you to help them learn skills to support it.

Fortunately, middle school is a prime time to let your child learn from poor choices because they have the opportunity to rethink, redo, and recapture ideas. Forgetting a homework assignment won't keep them out of Harvard Law School—they probably won't even fail the class. Yet, that reduced grade or zero can serve as a reminder, even a motivator, to pay attention to all those things that go into turning work in on time all the way down the pipeline to the final grade. And if your child missed making first chair in band because she left her French horn at home on the day of tryouts, the lesson is that she won't forget her instrument the next time. These logical consequences promote a deeper understanding of cause and effect. Ideally, mistakes like these lead to intrinsic changes. These are majestic opportunities for asking your child what they would do if they got a "redo."

Here it comes, the big idea, collaborative problem-solving. This process (which we'll discuss step by step in a moment) empowers your child to be the solution to their problems, and that generates ownership. It fosters trust and respect between you and your child. In addition, it promotes critical thinking, delayed gratification, and decision-making skills. Instead of just telling them what to do, you'll invite them to agree that a problem exists, come up with possible solutions, whittle down the possibilities to viable solutions, and empower them to follow through on what you agree to as a unit. While this is the exact foundational problem-solving you are already familiar with, the difference is that it is not from the top down; rather, it depends on all the stakeholders working together each step of the way.

A Leadership Philosophy Shift

As we discussed in Chapter 1, developing autonomy and identity are crucial tasks of adolescence, which means your child is eager to have a bigger say in their own life. For parents, however, this change requires a shift in how you think about your role as a parent. As the leader, the onus is on you to adjust your approach to your child.

When you collaborate with your child on solutions instead of simply telling them what to do, you provide freedom for them to voice their ideas, weigh choices, and make decisions. The autonomy therein provided meets the needs of the point in their development.

Thankfully, collaboration allows you to explore this power shift in small, practical steps. One of the first things parents can do to embrace this new leadership style is to shift from telling to asking. For example, instead of saying, "Go to bed!" (as Sam's parents were in the habit of doing), broach this topic in the form of a question: "What time did we decide on for lights out?" This technique works for many aspects of family life:

- Whose turn is it to walk the dog?
- Remind me what we decided about two Saturday chores.
- Tell me your plan for getting your project done.
- What day do you do your laundry?

When you reframe the conversation this way, you empower your tween to give voice to their plans. Instead of giving a litany of directions or advice, you give them the opportunity to explain their responsibilities and the steps they need to take to accomplish tasks. This makes it much more likely that your child will do everything they need to, because *they* voiced it.

So often as parents, we want to give our child everything, including instructions. We want to pour all of our knowledge, values, and wisdom directly into their hearts, heads, and hands. But at this age, just telling in many cases is not the best way to communicate. They spot the lecture coming and will tune it out in less than two sentences. I know this was mentioned earlier, but a reminder may be necessary. Lecturing is secondhand and not surprising, as we were on the receiving end from our own parents. Right now, your job is to watch and listen—and keep the faith that listening is actually the most powerful leadership skill you have at this point in your child's development. Less is more for sure in this case.

This shift requires some optimism on your part. As parents, we are often so anxious about our children's well-being that we don't want to let go of any control at all. To fully embrace collaboration—and to sell it to your child—you'll need to believe in yourself as the mentor and trailblazer. You are an initiator and catalyst who helps your child develop skills so they can reach their full potential. It is not about being the boss or doing the work. It is creating learning opportunities that tie you together.

It's normal to have doubts, but you can do this.

I hear these doubts loud and clear from parents all the time. You're probably thinking, *This all sounds great, but my kid* never *does the dishes/walks the dog/studies for tests without me nagging or nudging him. How can I believe that this time will be different?*

The answer is that you have to believe in your child and this process. When you're confident, your child will feel it.

Developing a Collaborative Mindset

Often, the most difficult part of collaborating is garnering agreement that a problem exists. Your eighth grader doesn't see his cursing as a problem, nor does your fifth grader see leaving Legos on the floor as a problem. When this is the case, your first challenge is to broach the issue in a way that doesn't immediately alienate your child. This requires you to reach out empathetically and emotionally. You can't *make* your child do anything, but you can *invite* them to solve a problem by showing them respect, recognizing a difficulty, and asking them to help you understand.

It's natural to want to dive into the problem and spout off about exactly how it's affecting you. One of my favorite clients loved to say to his tween daughter, "You're wrong, and I'll tell you why." She never wanted to have even a casual conversation with her dad. It's even worse than a lecture! Instead, collaboration begins with you being emotionally open. This isn't always easy to do, because it requires you to be vulnerable—and chances are you're already feeling raw from all of the conflicts.

What does it look like to invite your child to collaborate with you? Below are examples of healthy parent dialogue that illustrate a better way to set the table for collaboration.

Show Vulnerability

"James, every time we leave for soccer practice or a game, we have a problem. I yell at you. I threaten to not take you or not let you play. I feel bad. You must feel angry and frustrated, too. I suspect that you don't do as well as you could because I have upset you. I'm not proud of the way I treat you—the nagging and yelling. In fact, I'm embarrassed. I'd like to change the way we go to soccer. Would you be willing to talk with me about it?"

Because the dad takes ownership of his outbursts and threats, and acknowledges that he upsets James, the son sees another side of his dad: care, concern, and humanness. He recognizes his dad's regret and shame and his request that they look at the problem differently. The dad has created an opportunity using vulnerability and compassion to deal with getting to soccer. He is asking to move the issue from an emotional, right-or-wrong approach to talking about it easily. It's vulnerability and permission.

Show Understanding

"Mary, I've taken your phone away for two weeks this month. You work hard babysitting to pay half of the monthly fees. I'm sad that you haven't had your phone. I'm sure you miss being able to connect with your friends. I miss your funny texts. I'd like you to earn it back and keep it. Could we talk about how to make that happen?"

Without stating that Mary has failed to do whatever was required to earn her phone back—heavy emphasis on earning it back—her dad asks if they could chat about it. She's not in trouble, and he sincerely understands that this is hard for her.

Show Concern

"Milo, your science teacher emailed me about some missing homework assignments. I understand that science stresses you out. I know you do your homework, because you show it to me. I'm worried that missing homework grades will have an unwanted effect. I'm confused. Can you help me understand what happens to your homework?"

Stating facts and asking for an explanation with concern lets children know your interest and care is about them and their accountability.

Whenever a problem exists, your approach to solving it determines the likelihood of a peaceful transition for a positive solution. When you reach out expressing your emotions safely, stating your feelings honestly, and asking for your child's help genuinely, it's likely they will respond well. Feeling respected, cared about, and understood makes all the difference. They want your time and attention, and they need your humility and sincerity.

A Step-by-Step Approach to Collaboration

So, what does a collaborative approach to problem-solving with your child actually look like? I like to break it down into five distinct steps. Here's a link you can bookmark on your phone's web browser so you always have quick access to a refresher of these:
https://www.yourtweenandyou.com/steps-to-collaborating/.

1. Identify and Commit to Problem-Solving Together

Identifying the problem might seem obvious, but it's actually paramount to going forward. The first pact you'll make together is agreeing on what the problem actually is, and it sets the stage for the rest of the steps.

To do this, don't simply tell your child what you believe the problem is. Start by sharing your part in the problem and inviting them to share their position. Here are several well-designed prompts to get you started:

Express your concern with vulnerability. I'm wondering if we can talk about _____ (name the problem). I know that I let you down when I _____. Why is this a problem? I don't show you respect, and then we argue, and we both go away angry.

Who is this a problem for? Would you agree that this is a problem for both of us?

What are the benefits of solving this? We can learn how to work together and give each other the respect we deserve. Why will things be better? I believe in us, and I'd like us to talk about solutions we both agree on.

What has to be given up or given away, and is it worth it? I don't want to boss you around. I don't want to miss your game. I don't want to embarrass you in front of your friends. Would that be okay with you?

Can we agree to solve _____ together? This is the big ask, the invitation.

Express Gratitude. Thank you! I was hoping we could work this out together.

Once you agree about what the problem is, you can decide to solve it together. This initial agreement is the only way that collaboration will work. You've established a problem that you've both contributed to. Now you're forming a partnership that paves the way for the next steps.

2. Brainstorm Solutions and Respect All Ideas

Once you've agreed on the problem and on working together to solve it, it's time to look for possible solutions. This is an information-gathering process. At this stage, you don't want to assign any values to the suggested ideas, and you don't want to judge. Your job as the parent leader is to remain open to all possibilities—your suggestions and theirs.

To do this, ask your child to come up with solutions, and ask them to write the solutions down. Listen respectfully here, and resist the urge to dismiss anything out of hand. For example, suppose your child broaches a solution that involves giving all their chores to their younger siblings. This, of course, isn't an ideal resolution, and it may be worthy of a laugh—but now is not the time to cancel ideas. Allow them to add it to the list without comment, and let the ideas roll. It's good if you make suggestions, but don't pitch them as the ideal solution.

If you critique the ideas right away—or worse, start to argue about them—your child will shut down, and the whole process will grind to a halt. Brainstorming means accepting all ideas as equal possibilities for the moment. Also, when you model open acceptance of all that your child says, they will follow your lead without rejecting the ideas out of hand. This is an important first step in turning down the temperature of conflict and returning to a baseline of mutual respect.

One more thing: don't get yourself married to a single solution. It's necessary to be open-minded.

3. Sift through the Possibilities

Once all the ideas are on the table, it's time to explore them in more depth. You're still not going to dismiss ideas out of hand, however. Instead, encourage your child to think more deeply about the solutions by asking for more information. Here are some useful questions you can ask:

- What will that look like?
- Who will do what to make this happen?
- How long will this be in place?
- Will this work for _____?
- Is there a way to make this simpler?
- What aren't we considering?

You may also discover that you require more information about a solution to understand its full impact. For example, will a new chore schedule fit in with sports practices, scouts, or faith programs? If there are information gaps, let your child be the one to do the research and fit the new information into the proposed solution. This gives your child ownership while also allowing them to discover problems with the logic or fairness of their ideas—without you having to point it out to them. The power of their voice and insights makes the process even more valuable.

When you collaborate, everyone needs to be 100 percent invested in and committed to the solution. If you're not, you can explain your misgivings and ask more questions about getting to a solution that will work better. In this process, the key is to remember that value is added by disagreeing with the *idea*, not with the person who presented it.

4. Build Consensus and Solidify Ownership

As you consider all the possibilities, you'll eliminate some and zero in on others to come to an agreement that works for all parties. Then it's time to fine-tune your agreement so that everyone knows what's expected of them moving forward. This is the nuts and bolts of problem-solving, and it has several parts.

First, establish each stakeholder's role in the solution by outlining each person's responsibilities in making things work. Who's doing what and when under the new agreement?

Next, spend some time thinking about integration and execution. How will you and your child each support this solution and keep it going? It can be helpful here to review the benefits of the solution as a reminder of what's at stake and how your lives and relationships will improve. Two obvious examples are that you won't yell and he won't be yelled at. She won't stomp off mad and lose her phone. These kinds of examples are real to kids and us. It's more than okay to talk about them as benefits of collaborating. Children dislike conflicts even more than adults do.

Finally, it's time to express gratitude to your child for the solutions you've established. She needs to know you appreciate her abilities and commitment. And, that you've enjoyed this process.

5. Monitor Progress

Finally, you'll want to revisit your collaborative solution with your child to measure or evaluate that it's working. For parents who worry about things going wrong, this allows you to try the process's solutions. To prove that it does work or tweak it if not.

To do this, establish a date in the future when you'll sit down together to discuss how things are going. Maybe you enact your new solution for a week or a month and then schedule a talk over pizza. As life changes, new and better solutions may arise, so periodic check-ins with both team members provide the flexibility to keep making things better.

Remember that with tweens, change is fluid! Being proactive about evaluating how things are going gives everyone a chance to revisit and evolve. Your ability to adapt and collaborate will keep you and your child close during this time of rapid evolution—and if you make it a habit, you can find solutions together before things snowball into major clashes.

When Things Go Wrong

There will be days when the plans you make don't work. You may have reached an agreement about making the bed first thing or finishing homework before dinner. Things happen and nobody is perfect, but it's not time to cast blame or discipline. It's time to go back to the table together.

How you react when the shared collaborative plans and agreements are broken matters. Do you want to revert to nagging, cajoling, and coercing? No! And you don't have to. Because you've empowered your child to be their own leader, you can also turn to them for the solution to new problems.

Take a look at how collaborative communication continues to help families get past a temporary hiccup in their agreement about doing the dishes:

"Caitlyn, the dishes are still in the sink this morning. We agreed they would be in the dishwasher before bedtime on school nights," Ashley says when her daughter Caitlyn comes into the kitchen on Tuesday morning.

"I know, Mom. I'm sorry."

"Something must have happened."

"I was almost done with my report on Ruth Bader Ginsburg last night when that color wheel popped up. I had to force close the computer, and I couldn't get the document back. Chris tried too, and he couldn't get it either. I was so mad! It's due today, so I had to rewrite the whole thing. And then do all my math homework."

"That's so frustrating, honey," says Ashley.

"Right. So that's why the dishes aren't done. I am going to put them in the dishwasher now. I was too tired last night. Sorry, Mom."

"I understand. You were spent. Want some help?"

"Sure, thanks," says Caitlyn. "Mom, I need to remember to hit save every now and then. And maybe not cram so much in at the last minute."

"This has been a rough way to learn that. But now you've got it!"

Notice that Ashley did not say, "You didn't do the dishes. Again. You agreed to do them, and this is the third time this week you haven't followed through! What do you have to say for yourself?" Rather, she generously gave her daughter the benefit of the doubt, reached out to understand her, and offered her help. Above all, she remembered that the problem was the dishes not being done, not Caitlyn herself. Caitlyn is the solution.

Also, notice that Caitlyn reminded herself that she needs to save her documents as she types and not cram the night before something is due. Because emotional outbursts, blaming, and excuses weren't getting in the way, she had the opportunity to reflect and work toward solving additional problems.

Your commitment to holding it together when plans derail will serve to get things back on track easier. Being curious, rather than angry, about the details behind the failure keeps trust and respect alive—and opens the door for your child to take on additional responsibility for problem-solving in the future.

Collaboration in Action: Sam's Story

When Sam's parents came to me for help that day, I shared with them the five steps to collaborative problem-solving and walked them through how to apply the steps to their recurring bedtime argument. Let's return to Carrie, Greg, and Sam and observe how the parents shifted their strategy away from issuing demands and giving orders to collaborating.

First, Carrie and Greg had to shift their thinking to accept that the problem wasn't Sam. In fact, Sam was the solution. Only he had no idea. And the problem was bedtime. This is the issue that Carrie and Greg decided to focus on. That Saturday, Carrie began with the invitation, "Sam, we'd like to chat about how we do bedtime. Would you be willing to do that?"

At first, Sam was suspicious. His guard immediately went up because he knew that every time this topic came up, he ended up getting yelled at and punished. He dreaded this topic and the thought of a conversation about it already.

Then Greg offered, "We feel bad because we're always yelling at each other at bedtime. Most nights, you and I fight. I raise my voice and lose my temper. I threaten to take away your phone and time with your friends. I feel bad. You must feel angry and frustrated, too. Sometimes after we fight, the next morning I'm not even sure how to talk to you. It feels like you want to steer clear of us, too. I don't want to have those kinds of arguments anymore. I don't want it to come between us anymore."

Carrie added, "We're not proud of the way we treat you. In fact, we're embarrassed. We'd like to change the way we do bedtime. Would you be willing to talk with us about it?"

Greg and Carrie began this conversation with total honesty. They let themselves be emotionally vulnerable sharing their feelings. This openness and honesty softened Sam enough to listen.

"We'd like to do bedtime differently, and we need your help with that," Greg added. "We can't do it by ourselves."

"Really? You, want my help?" Sam was curious. "This is weird, but I guess it's okay."

"Thank you," Carrie smiled. "Can we agree to come up with a plan where none of us yell, and we don't go away angry at bedtime?"

"I guess that would be better," Sam conceded.

Next, Greg handed Sam a notepad and pencil. "Would you mind writing down the ideas we come up with for making bedtime different?"

Sam took the pencil and thought about it. "Well, I don't want a bedtime at all. I don't think I need one anymore because I'm not a little kid." Carrie and Greg just nodded while Sam wrote that down. Crucially, they did not interrupt Sam, judge, or correct his suggestion. And that is how brainstorming works—all ideas are considered viable.

Once Sam wrote down his ideas, he asked, "What about letting me decide the time? And what about not yelling at me?"

"Keep writing. You're doing well," Carrie added. "How about a specific time?"

"But I don't want a bedtime!"

"Yes, that's why it's on the list. All the ideas get to go on the list. Once we have all the ideas, we'll choose the ones that might work well. Fair enough, Sam?"

"I want to shower in the morning. So I'll put that on the list."

"Ok, what's next?" Carrie opened the door for Sam to give more input.

"No yelling, for sure."

"What else, Sam?"

"No bedtime. No punishments. No taking my devices."

"Please add a set bedtime to the list," Carrie added.

"Wait a second. I already said I don't want a bedtime."

"True enough, Sam, but everyone's ideas get to be on the list." They were teaching the process as they went along.

And so it went, until everyone's ideas were jotted down. Then it was time for step three, sifting through the possibilities. They reminded Sam that all three of them had to agree for collaborating to be effective. And they added that they wouldn't pressure or boss him, but they would all listen to each other.

Greg spoke first. "I can agree to control my temper. I won't yell at you."

"Then I won't either," said Sam.

"And we can take off losing my phone and iPad privileges?"

"I'm all for that!" Carrie chimed in, "and I feel that we need to have a set bedtime."

"Why? I don't."

"I think a plan will be easier for us to follow. Especially since we agreed to stay calm."

"I guess so." A reluctant concession from Sam.

Thoughtfully, Carrie suggested, "We don't really know how much sleep a twelve-year-old needs. Could you look it up, Sam?" Putting Sam in charge of the research gave him ownership and responsibility.

Sam returned and reported that kids his age need nine hours of sleep each night. "If I'm really supposed to get this much sleep, I'll add 'get nine hours of sleep' to the list."

"You know I'm not that good at math," Carrie admitted. "Sam, will you figure out the time for bed? You always get up in plenty of time to eat and catch the bus in the morning."

Finally, Sam said, "It looks like I need to get to bed by 9:00 to get enough sleep to be up at 6:00." He had chosen a bedtime for himself, and Carrie and Greg agreed.

"What else is left on the list, Sam?"

"No punishments."

"That's a goal for sure. We want to trust each other. Let's talk about what the 9:00 bedtime will look like, then."

Carrie started. "Will it mean heading to your room at 9:00? Reading for a while? Being in bed with the lights out? I think we'd feel better if we decide, so we don't fall into our old ways. What do you think, Sam?"

After some discussion, they agreed, and Sam voiced the plan. "I can head upstairs around 8:45, brush my teeth, and put the rubber bands on my braces. I can have the lights out by 9:00."

"That sounds good, Sam. May I add one more thing? I'd like to tuck you in." Greg was open emotionally.

"Like when I was younger, and you read me a story?" Sam grinned sideways.

"Yes. I'd like to have a moment to visit at the end of the day."

"Hmm, I never thought about that. I guess it'd be okay. But I don't need any kisses, Dad!"

Greg chuckled and replied, "Fair enough. Your mom or I will be in your room just before 9:00 to say good night."

"That sounds like a good plan," said Carrie. "I'm feeling better already. Will you talk me through it, Sam, so I'm sure of everything?"

Sam talked through the steps and then said, "Hey, Mom and Dad, this is just for school nights, right?"

"Good point. Yes," said Greg, and he added the final step. "Can we try it for the next three weeks, and then we'll talk about how it's going?"

This last part allowed each of them to track the progress and gave them all the flexibility to change bedtime in the future. They created the opportunity to renegotiate as circumstances change.

Key Takeaways

As they worked their way through the collaborative process for the first time, Carrie and Greg came to a major realization: Sam wasn't the problem. Sam was the *solution.*

This is true for your family as well. Your child is the *only* solution to getting their chores done, submitting homework on time, and going to bed at an agreed-upon time. You can yell and scream and try to force them, but your child has extraordinary power to obey or not—to struggle through conflicts or choose to acquiesce, or in this ideal case, collaborate with his parents.

As a confident parent-leader, you are a role model for your child to learn how you want to capitalize on that power and use it to build skills your child will use to become a competent adult with sound judgment. The sure way to do that is not to control and demand, but to invite solutions by making shared problem-solving strategies a way of life in your family. As you work through problems together as allies, partners, and equal decision-makers, you set shared goals, develop shared values, and build mutual trust and respect.

These are the life-changing gifts of collaboration.

Your Key Takeaways: Your Turn to Write

Name three things you learned.

1. _____

2. _____

3. _____

Name two awarenesses you'll embrace.

1. _____

2. _____

Name at least one thing you will apply. What will you do differently?

1. _____

☼✱✩☁⚡☾

Now that you've learned how to lead through collaboration, let's look at how we can apply this powerful new skill to help your tween develop even greater problem ownership and accountability.

Chapter 4
Ownership and Accountability! Who's Responsible?

F arah was in the den, playing with her youngest, when she heard her eighth-grade son, Hamid, enter the house.

"What on earth happened?" she called in greeting. "You studied so hard! You were so well prepared!"

"Huh?" Hamid looked confused as he shed his backpack and coat on the floor.

She looked up from the tower of blocks she was building with the toddler. "I looked at your grade online. You got a 74."

Hamid shrugged. "She hasn't handed them back to us yet."

Farah sighed as he headed toward his room. Hamid didn't seem to mind that his hard work and studying had produced a mediocre grade. His mom was tired of caring more about his education than he did. How could she get Hamid to take responsibility and hold himself accountable for his own future if he didn't care about his grades?

How, indeed?

Accountability: Ownership and Voice

Most parents can recognize Farah's exasperation. Tweens talk a lot about how they want more freedom and control over their lives, but they still act irresponsibly about the things we value and know are important in the short and long term. Farah would love to see Hamid take ownership of his grades, but whenever she tries to talk to him about how he is doing, he either changes the subject or complains she is nagging.

What Farah does not yet understand is that it's impossible for Hamid to take ownership of his education when his mother has already claimed it. She manages all the information. She knows more about his homework than he does. She reminds him of when things are due and even asks him what supplies he needs for projects. She asks for an explanation about his test scores before he can even process what he scored. This type of monitoring is so easy these days, thanks to grade portals and other online communication systems. Like many parents of middle schoolers, Farah uses these tools regularly, to the point that she is the expert, not Hamid.

Sadly, she is also usurping his voice—his story. Hamid is the one who studied. He is the one who took the test. He is the person who earned the grade. He is the one who the grade will impact. He is the one who knows the story of each grade. But his mom has made it about her: she has looked up the grade, and she has questioned what happened. She has defined a problem that she can't solve.

Just as Sam was the solution to the bedtime problem, Hamid must become the solution here.

Accountability is about teaching children how to take ownership of their responsibilities and discover the power of their voice, abilities, and work ethic. By handing over control to tweens in areas they can manage, such as grades and chores, parents can help them develop problem-solving skills, confidence, and resiliency—some of the most important required life skills.

These skills provide a major component of your tween's **Search for Identity**. As adolescents move from being taken care of to taking care of themselves, they are learning they are *capable*. This, in turn, instills confidence and empowers them to become their own person. Their voice becomes stronger as they begin to make their own decisions, find their own solutions, and establish their own priorities.

Leading your child through this shift is one of the most intense and necessary tasks of parenting. You are leading them to become their own person.

The One Who Owns the Problem Solves the Problem

It's easy to see the difference between ownership and accountability.

When we take on a new task, buy a new vehicle, or get a dog, we own this new thing. We engage with it, giving it our time and attention. A feeling of pride and satisfaction comes with the novelty and even the privilege of possession. Ownership is accepting that the care, maintenance, and performance lie with us. Ownership is fully accepting a new role.

Accountability is the responsibility for results and outcomes. Accountability is measurable. Each activity, action, and decision contributes to the consequences. We will train, walk, and feed the dog as well as see to its health and give it lots of love. We wash and gas up our car, see to its regular maintenance checks, and follow the rules of the road while driving it. Accountability is following through and being answerable for the effects. It comes after ownership.

As our children grow, we shift the ownership of age-appropriate tasks to them. Step by step, we prepare them for adulthood by teaching them new skills and how to solve their own problems. We anticipate the short- and long-range benefits. With each new role, their confidence and sense of self increase. When things don't go well, they can explore their actions to see what caused the blip and what needs to be done differently or tweaked next time. Let's look at doing their own laundry.

Giving your child the responsibility of doing their laundry begins with lessons on how to wash, dry, and fold their clothes. Perhaps there's a new laundry basket in it for them, too. Once they are proficient, they own the job and are accountable for keeping their clothes clean. It's easy to see how ownership comes first and accountability second.

Fast-forward to a Friday morning a month later. The band shirt they are supposed to wear to school that morning is stained and crumpled in the bottom of the clothes basket. The reasons for this oversight are not important at this juncture but are important later. For now, your tween must figure out how to approach and solve their dirty-shirt problem.

They own the problem because they own their laundry. They may consider these options: run it through the washer and dryer right now and wear it to school damp; spot-clean it by hand; wear it dirty and face the consequences; text the band director and ask to borrow a shirt; or ask Mom or Dad to wash it and bring it to school. You may not agree with the strategy they choose, and you can say no to being the solution. Letting your child crack the mystery is where the magic lies. It truly is *not* your problem. They own the problem, and they are accountable for the solution. You gave them ownership of their laundry because you knew they could master it.

Yes, there is discomfort and worry. We know emotions can run high and even feel overwhelming to our children. You may need to walk your child through accepting their emotions and moving on to problem-solving. This means engaging the cognitive portion of their brain.

We can be motivated by not wanting our child to suffer, feel bad, or have a negative consequence. That thinking, the fear and anxiety, is real. Yet when we consider the big picture and our goals for raising a confident problem-solver, we can't stand in the way of them learning the skills to support them. We have to let them have the consequences of their decision-making and actions.

I can give you a cautionary and true story about what can happen if we don't let our children have the benefits of learning accountability. These former tweens are adults today who were not given the opportunity to solve their own problems as children. Their parents were busy fixing everything so their child wouldn't have to deal with negative outcomes, uncomfortable emotions, and unwanted conflicts. But these now-adults missed out on learning the how-tos of adulting. They live on their parents' couches, unemployed, and not accountable for anything.

Those parents meant well, but it was their own emotions that kept them from being brave and courageous parents. I urge you not to be that parent. Believe that your children are capable—because they are.

Imagine them in the future, confident and capable adults taking care of all the things. You make this happen step by step.

It Will Be Okay

If, in the example above, your tween heads out the door in a damp shirt with a still-visible stain that a quick wash didn't fix, you might feel guilty for not helping. You might worry your child will be laughed at by peers or scolded by their coach. You might feel embarrassed by the idea of other parents seeing that shirt and judging you. You may even wish you could have put a sign on your tween saying, "I know it's dirty, but I'm teaching my child to solve their problems!" As hard as it may be to let your child stumble, however, it is necessary—and it will be okay.

Ownership requires choices, actions, and consequences to be real. Tweens need to follow through to be the masters of their universe and have true autonomy. Even when the aftermath is not ideal. Keep in mind that each event that is not what you or they wanted is a chapter in their growth—it's not the end of the book. The series of events all contribute to the end of the story.

As parent-leaders, we need to see that handing off responsibility and consequences is good, even when we play out the situation in our head and know ahead of time that our tween will end up (temporarily) miserable. You know that when they forget their lunch at home on Meatloaf Monday, they will have to eat a school lunch they hate, or else go hungry. When they come home and eat their after-school snack, that misery will disappear—and next time they might remember their lunch. That's where the learning happens.

You need not lecture or be punitive over the dirty team shirt or forgotten lunch. These are perfect examples of learning by logical consequences. No amount of lecturing is superior to the experiential learning going on inside them.

In fact, a great first step in passing off ownership is for parents who have spent years running an immediate delivery service—the forgotten saxophone, the required iPad, the needed cleats—to shut it down. In the short term, bringing your child's forgotten items ensures that they have everything they need, but in the long term, they are better off learning to make sure they have their possessions before they walk out the door each morning. The DoorDash parent hinders accountability, just like the "helicopter" parent who hovers to make sure they are present the second their child needs help, or the snowplow parent who clears every obstacle out of the way. Giving ownership to a tween empowers them, and it leaves the parent with more time to focus on the areas of their lives that belong to them.

Keep in mind that giving tweens ownership does not mean leaving them entirely on their own without support. For example, in our house, we have a "two school deliveries a year" rule, but exemptions happen...

In seventh grade, my son spent hours meticulously constructing a house out of sugar cubes and papier-mâché for a school project. He completed it on time and left it on the dining room table the night before so it would be safe and ready to transport to school the next morning. And then the next morning, he ran out the door without it. He had already used his two school deliveries for the year, but I still took the project to school. It was his intention that caused me to make an exception.

School is an obvious area where tweens have ownership. They attend and engage in class. They complete the assignments. They do the projects. They study for the test. They turn in the work. They follow the rubrics. They get all the credit and the opposite as well for their effort or lack of effort. Ownership gives them the chance for bragging rights, increasing confidence, and realizing cause and effect.

At the same time, education can feel like a scary area for parents to give tweens full control. How can it be okay to "let" your child fail a class or be moved out of an advanced level into a lower one? Putting their adult future into their very young hands may seem like a disastrous decision by a very poor leader.

The reality is that you will have less and less control over your child's education the older they get. As they move from middle school to high school, it will become harder to know every teacher and to check over every homework assignment, especially as their courses become more advanced. (Exactly how much chemistry or world history do you remember?) They will be given opportunities in class to make decisions on what project they will work on and will rely on notes they take during lectures you never hear. The best thing you can do is start preparing them for that greater independence now by instilling the idea that their education is ultimately their own. You will still stay involved by asking questions and giving support, but the shift in ownership will empower your tween in a very necessary way.

When your tween takes ownership of their education, you may be able to predict that their decision to leave a homework assignment until the next morning will mean it doesn't get finished, which will mean a low grade, which will mean being benched for the next basketball game. That will be painful for your child. It might even be painful for you. But that pain is okay. One mistake does not turn your child into a failure. Instead, it's an opportunity to learn and do things differently next time.

An added benefit is that life gets more pleasant for everyone when tweens take ownership. When parents own the grades and act like those grades are their responsibility, they end up as the bad guys, nagging and yelling and losing it. Parents hate it, and children hate it more. But when responsibility shifts and when parents pass off ownership, they don't have to be the bad guys anymore. Tweens become their own bosses—free to nag or not nag themselves as much as they want.

Handing off ownership to our child does not mean we hand off leadership. We are still watching and monitoring. We are still 100 percent invested in our child's learning. We are still very much influencing, inspiring, and empowering them.

For example, consider how leadership works in a car factory. As a director of operations, you have many line workers under you. You ensure a safe and usable factory for them. You secure the contracts for steel, computer chips, and other necessary materials. You provide all they need to do their jobs. But you, yourself, are not running the machines that shape the steel. You are not inserting the electrical wiring. The line workers are doing that. You make sure the big needs are met so the line workers can do their own jobs. You facilitate, not micromanage, so that the cars can be built.

At home, you will also be the leader when it comes to your tween doing their schoolwork. You create a safe environment for studying, with time and space to work. You set the expectations for success and provide the freedom for them to do their work without micromanaging, fixing, or taking over. Your children are the ones who need to do the learning, but your leadership and belief in them is essential.

Accountability Builds Identity and Voice

When tweens have ownership of and accountability for key things in their lives, they secure the power to develop their own identity and voice. The power of voice emanates from the internal and external. Our internal voice chatters all the time, feeding us information: *good job here; you could have done better there; don't worry about missing that one thing on the timeline; you're human; remember to do the thing; don't be late; that joke was funny; I wish I'd studied more; I better get gas; I'm relieved I spoke to her; he is a nice guy; I'm not sure if playing the piano matters to me anymore—will my parents let me stop taking lessons?*

And on and on.

The outer voice, the spoken words, is more than telling stories or anecdotes about us. It's our platform for verbal self-expression and communication. It's asking for what we need, conveying our intentions and feelings, sharing an opinion or idea, leading a group, giving a speech. It's our narrative that portrays us, our personality, mood, and attitude.

The internal and external voices come together as tweens grasp and grapple with who they are and what they value.

Problem-Solving and the Development of Identity

Even if it seems easier at the moment for parents to control things for their children—to say, "Let's just get it done"—that plan will backfire in the long term. We need to help tweens build mastery. That happens by practicing.

The series of small steps taken on the road from childhood to being a capable, kind, and educated adult matter. So, we give our tweens help and opportunities to develop strong habits that they can apply not just to homework and laundry but to current and future challenges or adversities: a relationship fails, they are rejected after trying out for a team, they lose their phone, or they miss a deadline. They are developing the internal voice that will help them become a successful adult.

This internal voice is very powerful. Instead of fretting, thinking *Oh no, I messed up* or *I'm embarrassed*, we want our kid to say to themself, *Here's a problem, and I can solve it.* Instead of panicking and instantly calling you for help, we want our kid to stay calm and think through their options: *I can figure this out. What is the first step? What resources do I need? I need to breathe first. Is this a situation where I can just gut it out, even if I'm uncomfortable?*

As that internal voice of confidence grows stronger with additional success, it becomes a fundamental and core belief in their growing identity. From each experience they gain the muscle memory of figuring out their own solutions when dealing with a stain on their team shirt, losing their notes for the open-book test, or passing the ball to the wrong player. They can master their universe.

This confidence triggers intrinsic motivation: *I know I can solve my own problems* becomes *I want to solve my own problems* and even *I want to plan ahead to avoid problems.* The desire to succeed also becomes part of their identity.

They become more capable, accomplished tweens by learning problem-solving habits, even though sometimes those lessons aren't pleasant. As their identity forms and builds, from your vantage point, it's rewarding to observe its metamorphosis.

Building a Strong Voice

This development of identity/voice is not just something that happens in a crisis. It also happens when our child succeeds. As parents, we need to remember that we do not own our children's failures—and we do not own their successes, either.

Sometimes I encounter parents who aren't clear about who owns their children's success stories:

Outside school before the first bell, I say good morning to Min and her dad, Jung. Min bounces over to me with a spring in her step. "I had so much fun at the soccer tournament this weekend!"

"I'd love to hear about it."

Min's eyes widen, and she rocks on her feet as she begins. "Well, it was the championship game, and we were ahead by one goal with less than a minute left. The best player on the other team got the ball on a breakaway and—"

Jung interrupts. "All the parents got to their feet and started shouting. We didn't want the other team to tie! And then suddenly Min was running down the field, chasing her down. I was yelling, 'Go Min!' so loudly I was hoarse after. And just when this player was going to shoot, Min gained on her and sent the ball back to our players! And we won! All the parents were hooting and hollering. We were so proud of our daughters and winning!"

Jung pats his daughter's shoulder. "You were great," he says.

"Thanks," Min answers, but her eyes are no longer bright, and she's standing still.

"See ya." Min lets out a sigh as walks into the building.

As much as we can understand Jung's delight in his daughter and the win, he totally steals Min's thunder when he verbally takes over describing the game. More than that, he takes Min's story and makes it about him and how he and the other parents felt. He eliminates her voice and her ownership of the victory.

Consider how Min herself might have told the story instead:

Min's eyes widen as she shifts her weight from one foot to the other. "Well, it was the championship game, and we were ahead by only one goal with less than a minute in the game. The best player on the other team got the ball on a breakaway, and I was the closest defender, so I knew it was up to me. We'd practiced tackling from behind all last week and remembered exactly what Coach Jeffery had said to do and not do. I knew if I did it wrong, she could have gotten a penalty kick, and that would've been so unfair to Emma—she's our goalie. She's really good."

Min takes a big breath and continues talking faster and faster. "The other player was much bigger than I am. She looked over her shoulder and saw me coming, and she kept dribbling. There was no one to pass to. And her footwork was so good! I heard people yelling, but I didn't know what they were saying. I just kept running and trying to angle in on her, and then she stumbled a second, and that's when I gained on her and did a slide tackle—like this!" Min tilts her body and sticks out her right leg.

"Only, like, I'm sliding my whole body on the ground! I'd never done that in a game before! But I got the ball away, and I didn't foul her, and then our center, Maria, took it back down the field, and then the whistle blew, and we won! My whole team hugged me, and Coach told me she was so proud of how calm and focused I was."

Min's grin is huge. "I think I might even be able to make the team when I'm in high school!"

When Min tells the story, it's entirely different. She focuses on what she thought and felt, on how she handled a tricky situation. She reviews her play almost step by step. We can hear her confidence and planning— we can hear *her*. By telling her own story, Min gets to tell us who she is. The risk she was going to take. She is someone who can strategize a plan and follow through. She pays attention, works hard, and cares about her team. Through her voice, she experiences the ownership of her story and her success, and she asserts her identity.

We recognize the strong feelings we have for and about our child and how we believe in them. And this is a good thing and necessary. Our kids need us to believe in them. But how they feel about themselves, their abilities and strengths, and their choices and outlook matters even more.

Sharing Your Vision with Your Child

In our families, we create a vision of what we believe life should look like. Part of it could be that our children wake up every day and go to school, do homework and chores, and eat dinner with the family. It could involve participating in scouting or community theater, raising horses, hunting, or gardening. This vision is based on our values, which are embedded in all that we do as a family. Those values could also include religious faith, kindness, consideration, hard work—whatever they are, they are at the heart of that vision.

As parents, we want our children to continue to hold our values as they grow up—to adopt our vision of what life should look like. We hope they will take ownership of those values. During the tween years, we know they will question everything about what they do and what their family does: *I hate going to church/temple/the mosque! Hiking is so stupid. Why do we have to have a big dinner with our cousins every month?*

They may rebel against our values and reject our family vision, at least for a while.

As parents, we want to provide continuous care. We want to maintain our vision and continue sharing it, even as our tweens begin to push away or explore other options. We should continue to do activities that are deeply important to us and continue to invite our tweens to join us. They might accept the invitation or not. They might change the way they participate so it is not exactly the way we do it. This is how they develop their own values and vision. In this case, we are not handing off ownership but modeling what ownership of a life vision means.

How to Shift Ownership

Shifting ownership to your tween will not happen all at once. They may also struggle, especially at first, with their new roles. But following these steps will make the process easier.

Pick Areas That Make Sense for Your Child

There are many areas where tweens can take over responsibilities. Look for things that affect them directly, such as the habits that lead to success in school, making their bed each morning, keeping their room clean, monitoring their own screen time, giving away things they no longer use or clothes they've outgrown, and keeping their backpack in order. You can also look for things that contribute to the household, such as mowing the lawn, taking out the trash, making the grocery list, cleaning the bathroom, doing dishes, and setting and clearing the table.

Start Small

You've already handed off many tasks to your child, so you are on track. Set your tween up for success by beginning with an area that will be easy for them to master, or ask them to help you with individual parts of a larger task. Add on more when they demonstrate proficiency.

Discuss the Benefits of Ownership

Because tweens want independence but also recognize the luxury of having a parent do things for them, they may need some convincing that having duties is a good thing. For example, why should they start to change their own sheets when Mom does a marvelous job? Explain that additional tasks are not a punishment but a recognition of their maturity and getting them prepared for adulting. Plus, you know it's your job to hone their skills.

Pass On the Tools

Give your tween the necessary tools, information, and skills they will need when they take on a new task. This demonstrates your belief that they are capable of the task. With the laundry example above, you can give them a laundry basket and teach them three lessons: how to load and run the washer, how to load and run the dryer, and easy ways to fold or hang their clothes. They will then have a skill set they can use for the rest of their lives.

Demonstrating how to do certain tasks works for many areas. For other areas, more collaboration will be required. For example, when you place your tween in charge of tracking their own grades, you will want to set up a time to discuss with them what that switch will look like. Ask them to brainstorm what the new system will be. How often will they check their grades? How and how often will they keep you informed? When will you discuss any problem areas? Remember to keep judgment of their school performance out of this conversation.

Start Where Your Child Is

Recognize that you will need to meet your child where they are in the moment and build from there. Not all tweens are able to perform at a high level at school or at every household task, so you will need to have reasonable expectations. Also, as we learned in Chapter 1, your tween is still developing their executive functioning skills, so they may struggle in some areas, such as organization or planning, and be inconsistent in others. We need to accept their abilities—and potential—for what they are, and keep in mind that we are giving them an opportunity to achieve more. This translates to building confidence and self-assuredness.

A Note about Patience

No matter how carefully you plan and train for handing the ownership of a new task to your tween, they will make mistakes. This is a learning process that takes time, and some skills will be harder to master than others.

For example, a child who has issues keeping their papers and backpack organized will benefit by learning how. You can teach them to go through their backpack on a set afternoon each week and either throw papers away or put them where they belong. You can ask them how this technique will be beneficial now and later. They will always want a reason, and if they see the purpose, it's easier. It can take significant time for some tweens to build organizational skills, sometimes with two steps forward and one step back. Sometimes baby steps are necessary.

The next step could be to encourage them to organize their papers into their folders at the end of each class, or day, and so on.

However, for some children, the once-a-week backpack check may be too much to take on. For instance, my son is one of those kids who is not naturally organized. One year, he had a teacher who required her students to keep all their papers in order for each marking period. She gave them the tools to do it—a list of what they should have, what order they should be in, holes already punched in the papers—but over time, the number of papers really built up.

My son kept all the papers he needed to keep, but he shoved them inside of his backpack, all crinkled, crumpled, or wadded up. The day before they were due, he would take them out, iron them out with his hands on his bed, and put them in order in his folder. I could not bear to watch this laborious process, but I didn't have to—it was *his* schoolwork. That system worked for him, but as the year went on, I noted, "It takes you an hour and a half to get those papers ready each time. What could you do differently?"

He decided to try to keep his papers in a folder instead. And at the end of the next six weeks, half of the papers were in that folder, and half of them were loose and crumpled in his backpack. But that was measurable progress.

The lessons tweens must learn to successfully take ownership are not always quick or easy. We can train them and take the right approach. We can cheer them on. But the transition does not happen overnight.

What can seem straightforward for us can seem complicated and confusing for kids. We can help, and we can be their leaders, but we can't do it for them. Even if they stumble, however, the answer is not to take back ownership. That stumbling is all part of becoming resilient to solve the problem and becoming accountable.

Accountability in Action: Hamid's Story

Let's return to Hamid and his mom, Farah, from the beginning of this chapter. She knows she can alter the dynamics around Hamid's grades by passing the ownership of his grades to him. Let's see how that could work.

The next day, when Hamid comes home from school, Farah waits for him at the kitchen counter with his favorite snack. "Your brother's taking a nap, so get yourself settled, and then I'd like us to chat. Don't worry, you're not in trouble."

Curious, Hamid puts his things away and joins his mom. "Are we going skiing next weekend?"

"That's not it. But I'd like your help. The truth is, I've been in charge of guiding you through school for a long time. I've been looking at that grade portal for years and asking you a zillion questions about assignments, projects, due dates—you know I nag you. And now I'd like to stop. I'll still be involved in your education. I'll still read your teacher's emails. I'll still help you with studying whenever you ask. But I want to learn about your grades, test dates, and so on from you. I'd like you to take charge."

Hamid laughs. "Mom, there's no way you're going to suddenly stop checking my grades and bugging me about school."

She grins. "I am, because I also want us to work together to come up with a plan for you to tell me about what's going on grade-wise. Are you willing to do that?"

Hamid takes a sip of his drink and thinks. "I mean, are you sure you trust me to handle all that?"

"Yes," Farah nods. "Absolutely. It's way past time. You are the one who does all the work and knows all the things. So, how do you think we could do this?"

Hamid and Farah brainstorm and talk through various ideas. At the end of their collaboration, they have a plan in place.

"Okay," Hamid says. "So, on Thursdays after dinner, we'll sit here in the kitchen, and I'll show you my grades for the week, class by class, on my iPad. And if I'm worried about any of them, I'll explain why, and you'll keep a list of any ideas we come up with. I'll look at my overall averages ahead of time and tell you if any are below 85." He opens his iPad to the grade portal. "Like in science, remember? That test score was below 80, so I can retake the test, and that should pull it back up—if I can keep mitosis and meiosis straight this time." He lightly slaps himself on the forehead.

Farah smiles, amazed at her son's enthusiasm. "Sounds good. And what did we decide about English since that teacher doesn't post grades very often?"

"Oh yeah. I'll hold on to all my papers with grades for that class, and I'll show those to you. Will that work?"

"Yes. Good thinking. What else do you think?"

"I think it'll work," he grins. "It's weird that she doesn't put her grades in, since she is so strict about everything in that class. Did I tell you what she does when kids start talking? She stops what she's doing, stares at them, and says, 'I'll wait.' And it totally works, even though she's this tiny woman!" Hamid gets up and imitates his teacher, rocking back and forth on his heels with his hands clasped behind his back, looking sternly at his mom.

Farah feels like she has learned ten new things about her son during this conversation. By the end, Farah can readily see how giving her son ownership of his grades will transform his attitude and maybe even his performance. His willingness to take charge and his insights on the best ways to share information indicates he is ready for this shift. Farah must trust the new process and agreement, and not look at the portal.

Second-Tier Learning

We barely touched on the huge value of learning from an experience that didn't go well. Say your child puts in the time studying for a four-chapter history test. He knows the dates, people, and background. And you know he knows the information, because he asked you to quiz him. Yet he comes home from school with a sour look, and dreadful words pour out of his mouth.

"The test sucked, and I'm sure I failed."

Of course, you want to give assurances and dissipate his pain. But you know better. Instead, your response is empathetic. "I hear your disappointment. This isn't the outcome you expected."

"No. It was an essay test. He wanted us to write about the causes of the Civil War."

"That had to be hard to deal with."

"Yeah. All I could remember was slavery. I know there is more to it. But I don't know what it is."

"It's frustrating when you can't think of the answers."

"Yeah. Now I have to figure it out."

"I believe you will."

Huge things happened here. The mom didn't rescue him from his feelings or tell him it would be okay, or express her own personal or emotional response. She listened to understand him, let him deal with the facts, and defined his emotions for him. It wasn't about the results of the Civil War exam. His mom was present for him.

She let him own the problem and gave him 100 percent support. He may end up learning how to better prepare for tests and how to look at the big picture, not just data, or he may learn how to draw conclusions from inferences.

Key Takeaways

When we give children ownership of their lives, step by step, they get to be accountable for the results. By handing over control to tweens in areas they can manage, such as grades and chores, parents help them develop problem-solving skills, confidence, and resiliency.

Developing accountability in our tweens requires parents to understand that their children have the ability to solve their own problems, and that they should feel comfortable trusting them to do so. Tweens won't be perfect. They are a work in progress, but they deserve the opportunity to try their best and learn from their mistakes—without having their parents jump in immediately to save the day or point out their deficiencies. As parent leaders, we provide the time and the tools and ultimately leave our children to do the important work of growing up and becoming remarkable young adults.

Your Key Takeaways: Your Turn to Write

Name three things you learned.

1. _____

2. _____

3. _____

Name two awarenesses you'll embrace.

1. _____

2. _____

Name at least one thing you will apply. What will you do differently?

1. _____

☼-✱✩◌϶☾

Teaching our tweens ownership and accountability is are also important when it comes to their own changing bodies. These lessons will lay a crucial foundation for issues relating to sex, love, and relationships, which we'll cover next.

Chapter 5
Sex, Love, and Relationships—the Trifecta Parents Fear the Most

After eleven-year-old Caleb went upstairs to bed, he realized he left his homework in the den. As he collected it downstairs, he could hear his parents, Michelle and Dean, in the kitchen talking about his beloved summer babysitter, Grace, who was away for her sophomore year of college.

"Her mom told me today that Grace is five months pregnant!" he heard his mom say.

"That's unexpected," Dad answered. "Is she going to stay in school?"

"I don't know. Her boyfriend's graduating in May, so I hope he's able to find a good job. Grace's parents won't be able to support them much."

"They're so young. Raising a baby was hard enough for us, and we'd planned everything out and were married for five years."

"I hate to say it, but this seems like a poor and stupid decision for Grace." Caleb was surprised by the tone of his mother's voice. She made

Grace sound bad.

"Agreed." His dad sounded just as upset. "Sometimes I think college students now think the whole point of being there is to have as much sex as possible."

"Well," Mom said with a laugh. "As I recall, there was a whole lot of sex back in our day too."

Caleb entered the room. "Grace is super smart—she got that big scholarship. Why would you say she's stupid?"

"Caleb!" Mom snapped. "You know better than to listen in on conversations that aren't meant for you."

"Why is it such a big deal that she has sex?" He noticed Mom's face was so red. "She's a grown-up. You said sex was okay for grown-ups."

"This isn't a good time," Dad looked at him sharply. "Just go to bed."

"Why is having a baby so bad?"

"Please, go to bed." He heard his mom's anger and frustration. Caleb did as he was told but had trouble falling asleep. He had so many questions, and it was clear to him his parents didn't want to answer them. They had given him the "sex talk" last year, but there was still so much that confused him. Good thing he knew that eighth grader on the bus. That guy would answer his questions the next day.

Be the Parent They Need

Parents look forward to sharing and teaching their children family stories, games, music, and hobbies. Usually, teaching them about sex is not one of things we look forward to. We come with so many assumptions, biases, and uncertainties that being calm and confident talking about sex with our children seems impossible. We feel nervous, uncomfortable, and unsure. Yet, discussing not just sex but also love and relationships falls on the list of parental responsibilities.

We all have our own stories of how we learned about sex. They left an impression—both being informed or not. Contrary to what you may believe as truth, your kids want to hear about it from you. They want you to be honest and straightforward. This makes you the best person to tell your child everything about sex, love, and relationships. As such, it is essential that you find reassurance in your role and an ease in your conversations.

Your goal needs to be to communicate openly and honestly, as well as frequently, so your child understands and knows what to expect. Your conversations will not be limited to the facts of reproduction and the mechanics of the sex, but will include healthy relationships, safety, pressures, identity, consent, and so much more. Your child needs your help and insight navigating this life change. And they need each body part to be called its real name—a penis is a penis, breasts are breasts, a period is a period, etc. One of the major benefits will be witnessing your child's comfort and confidence when they come to you with their questions and concerns.

It's a relief that talking about this is not a one-and-done event. Their questions and ability to understand will evolve as will the level of trust and respect that grows between you. The only way to make sure those conversations continue to happen is to create a safe environment for them. You can do this.

As we saw in Caleb's story, sometimes children ask questions we are not prepared for, and they often ask them at times when we are not at our best. We also saw in Caleb's story that kids have acute antennae for reading their parents' comfort level talking about different subjects. For example, they know Dad loves talking about the Giants and laughs when you tease him about being bald, but if you mention that disastrous trip to Washington, D.C., he folds his arms across his chest and stares above your head. Mom will talk all day about how she used to play the clarinet, but if you bring up the speeding ticket she got on the way home from the piano recital, she presses her lips together and narrows her eyes. Tweens figure out quickly which subjects are safe to talk about with you.

It makes sense that you overcome your discomfort talking about reproduction, sex, hormones, pubic hair, periods, wet dreams, and pregnancy. You want to be the one they come to with questions because an informed, trustworthy, caring parent is their best source of factual information and guidance—not a peer or someone who may not share your deep knowledge of your child and the values you wish to impart.

Or the internet. Your leadership skills as an empathetic and honest communicator, listener, and guide support your role.

Thinking about your first sexual awakening will help you focus on your child. I'm not advocating that you **ever** share any of your experiences with your child; besides, they will 100 percent not want to hear them. But you've experienced things they have not—so for once, you are more informed than they are.

Do Your Research and Know Your Terms

In order to be that informed parent, you might need to do some research. You need to know not just how the human body works but also what terms to use and how to explain everything clearly.

Most adults have a general idea about how the fallopian tubes release an egg, how a sperm reaches it, fertilization, embryo, fetus, and baby. You know the bodily changes in pregnancy and birth, and the reality of a baby to raise. You may have even covered this information by the time your child hits the tween years. Which is the ideal scenario. If not, you can catch up now.

When you have these conversations, be sure to cover both male and female development. Sometimes parents tell sons what happens to boys and tell daughters what happens to girls, but in fact, tweens need to know what happens to both sexes. Tell your sons that girls grow breasts and that it's not painful. Tell your daughters where boys grow hair and what an erection is. And all the other things. Teaching about sex from all perspectives will give your tween the information they need to make decisions for themselves and to be respectful of others. Knowledge provides a solid base. Having the correct information does not make them more or less likely to engage in sex.

If you are having a planned conversation, organize your thoughts and even practice what you are going to say so that you will be as comfortable as possible during the actual discussion. Envision yourself being calm and confident. Also, plan what you want your child to take away from it. What are your goals? Start finding the right time and letting them know you have information you want to share with them.

Be ready for questions along the way—gauge your child's age and respond appropriately. And be ready for no comments or lots of questions. Stay calm. Any anxiety you have will bleed to your child. They don't want you to feel uncomfortable, and the reverse is true, too.

For both planned and unplanned conversations, your job is not just to give information but to make sure your child understands. You can do this by asking them open-ended questions or prompting statements like "You may have wondered about this, eh?" or "Maybe you know about this already, but…" or "What seems confusing?" The empathetic responses we discussed in Chapter 2 will be helpful here to keep the conversation going: "I know this is a lot." "It may seem overwhelming." You also want to give your tween ample time to think about what was mentioned and then listen carefully to everything they say. Make it clear that this is a topic the two of you will chat about a lot—it will be an ongoing process and an ongoing conversation.

Above all, remember that this is a conversation not just about sex but about your tween's heart, emotions, and imagination. It's extremely personal because it's their body and the increasing awareness of themselves as a sexual being with roles. You are teaching your precious child, who, like a caterpillar, will go through a monumental metamorphosis. I know you'll treat them and the subject with thoughtful kindness and gentle care—and maybe a little awe.

Sex Feels Good

The fact that sexual contact is pleasurable is often the most daunting aspect of talking about sex with your children. Too often, pleasure gets ignored or buried rather than presented as the truth of a wonderful basic feature. And its excitement goes unmentioned. Your reliability increases with your honesty.

I bet you can recall your first sexual awakening with another person. Here's Kathy's story:

> The summer I turned thirteen, I attended a church dance with my best girlfriend. She introduced me to a guy named Bob. We talked and danced all evening. It was

enchanting. Bob fascinated me. As the last dance was announced, he took my hand, placed his other hand on the back of my neck, and asked if he could kiss me. I said yes. Then, off and on during the dance, he kissed me softly on my lips. He was sweet and gentle. I felt a fire luxuriating in my pounding heart. Every cell in my being tingled with excitement. Something more potent, more exhilarating than I ever encountered, raced through my body. That surge of electricity—its intensity—thrilled me. I felt a power, a strength I'd never felt or even imagined. Those kisses opened the door to my sexuality. I loved it. I wanted to feel this wonderful and excited all the time.

Tell your children the truth and the reality—that sex feels good (or *should* feel good). If we omit that fact and only warn them about the risks of unplanned pregnancies and sexually transmitted infections (STIs), we risk undermining our credibility about everything else we say because we've left out crucial and relevant information. No matter what we do or say, they are going to become sexually mature human beings and learn without you. Nature always has its way.

We worry what will happen if our children know this information. We need to choose what to communicate not out of fear but for our child's benefit and preparation. If we tell our child sex is fun, they will not automatically go out and have sex. And if we tell them sex can harm them, they will not automatically avoid sex until they are thirty. As the holder of all the facts and a trusted resource, you must accept the benefit of giving them the full picture. Biologically, sex is for procreation. Sex has risks. It is also designed to feel good and be fun.

Some readers may disagree with this idea, so let me take it a little further. The reality is the majority of parents have sex in their house with their partners. Your child may have even walked in on you. But sex, by and large, has been your secret. When we let our children in on the secret that sex feels good, we may feel like we don't own that secret anymore. Nevertheless, your child is going to find out eventually, so you have two options. You can either reveal that secret yourself, or you can have them learn it from a less reputable source.

In other parts of the world, such as in Scandinavia, sex is not stigmatized as it is in the United States. These countries also have lower rates of teen pregnancy and sexually transmitted infections than the US, suggesting that young people are better off when we don't treat sex as a bad, dangerous, or off-limits topic. Any leftover Victorian attitudes you may possess may not benefit you or your tween.

Talking about Romantic Relationships

Discussions about romance and relationships are encased in values. At one point, you might have talked to your child about what qualities they like in their friends. Do you want a friend who is outgoing? Kind? One who keeps your secrets? Who studies? Who believes what you believe? Who challenges you? A good listener? Who will invite you to their birthday party?

Similarly, when we talk about romantic relationships, we again want to talk about what our child is looking for in a boyfriend or girlfriend. You can have easy discussions about how they see themselves, and what qualities they value and want in a boyfriend/girlfriend relationship, and what they want to receive and give. You can include practicing how they'd stand up for themselves about what they do and don't want, and being able to speak freely about their feelings, hopes, and dreams. You want them to have a strong and kind voice. Navigating and looking inside relationships doesn't come naturally.

The thing is most tweens don't consider these things consciously. Their **Prefrontal Cortex** is not developed enough to conceptualize the parameters of a friendship or romantic relationship. But they still have expectations. For example, if they send a text, they might expect a reply from a friend immediately. Or they may be fine with some people not responding for a couple of days. Expectations become more complicated in romantic relationships. Will they expect a romantic partner to reserve every Friday and Saturday night to be together? If they kiss someone, does that mean they expect that person not to kiss anyone else? How will they communicate their expectations to their partner? Later, if they have sex, will they expect their partner not to share that information?

We want to help our tweens figure out what qualities are important to them. How they want to be shown affection or closeness. Are their preferences for fun the same? Do they have the same educational plans? How do they show respect to others? Are they slobs or neatniks? Do they understand consent and respect it? We need to let them know that they don't have to give up anything or pretend to be different so that a particular someone will like them. In our culture, girls, in particular, can fall into the trap of molding themselves to please a partner or focus on making another person happy at the expense of remaining true to herself.

When we talk to tweens about relationships, it's important to ask them to think about qualities and behaviors. What do they need from the other person? What do they want to give? We want them to realize that the needs of both people should be honored. If you have a faith system, it may help you guide your child through these discussions. You may have heard some version of these famous words from the Bible: "Love is patient. Love is kind. Love is not self-seeking." This is a great learning tool. I'm sure there are many others.

These discussions also help your child figure out what they value in *themselves*, in addition to what they would value in a romantic partner. In response to your open-ended questions and ongoing willingness to discuss relationships, your tween might tell you something like the following:

- "I'm a person who swears when I'm frustrated. But I don't want a partner who does that because I would feel disrespected."
- "I'm a person who follows through on things. If I have a school assignment, I turn it in on time. If I have a chore, I get it done before I play my video game. It'd drive me crazy to have a boyfriend/girlfriend who is unreliable."

These conversations can be eye-opening for kids. They might not realize that their habits emerge from their values, or even the reverse, but your leadership in this area can help them understand what they want from themselves and from others—and why.

A great way to open this conversation is when you are watching a show or a movie together. You can express curiosity about a character, especially when the character is a tween or teen. Then ask your child what they think, how they see it, how they think it felt for the characters, and if they would have done the same thing. And you can delve further into the plot by asking, "What do you think they wanted when they did that, or what other choices they had?"

Ask with pure curiosity rather than out of any morality or looking for a particular answer. Don't say, "If it were me, I would have done this..." Avoid lecturing; the goal is for your tween to put themselves in the situation and think critically. You can also focus particularly on the motives behind behavior by asking, "I'm wondering why they did that?" Be careful to avoid being judgmental. Your goal is to open your child's eyes about how the characters respond to each other, their opinion, and alternatives. And how it translates to them. An added bonus is that you get to learn about your child.

This process is called **values clarification**. It asks your tween to identify and define what they value. It is about their beliefs in everything—their faith system, their work ethic, and their willingness to look at things from other points of view, even their self-concept. Values clarification is a self-reflection exercise for figuring out who they are and how they tick. It is a lifelong process because change is constant. Through this process, tweens can start to understand their principles and preferences. At some point, it will become apparent these things are their core and direct how they interact in their world.

It's hard: in their **Search for Identity**, tweens are already busy trying to figure out who the heck they are. And it's even more of a stretch for them to think about what they want from someone else, except to have a sense of being liked or even loved. But the goal is not for them to make concrete decisions about their lives—you are not asking them to submit a report to you labeled "Ten Things I Want in a Spouse." Instead, it's about giving them food for thought—ideas to process over time.

Then, when your child is asked to homecoming or prom by a person who is intriguing, funny, and smokes weed before and after school, they can decide how to respond to the invitation based on what they want in a person. Do they want the intriguing and funny parts? Do they want the weed-smoker so they can try it too, or is that a deal-breaker based on what they value?

No matter how much we talk with our children openly and honestly, when it comes to sex and dating, adolescents sometimes make impulsive choices or fail to think about the consequences. Remember, their **Immature Prefrontal Cortex** can't be counted on to look objectively. Some of their choices can lead to harmful outcomes, physically or emotionally. They may perform a sexual act that brings them no pleasure. They may get an STI. They may hurt their partner's feelings. They may spend two weeks in constant anxiety wondering if they are pregnant or got someone pregnant.

Values clarification does not prevent bad things from happening. But it can help teach our children to avoid sexual or romantic choices that are tempting, exciting, and alluring that could net negative results. They might not always make the healthy or wise choice, but they will have a framework for making their choices and perhaps analyzing why a particular choice turned out good or not so good. This helps them make decisions about what they want the next time.

Safety, Self-Respect, and Respect for Others

Safety, self-respect, and respect for others are among the most crucial topics to address. Your tween has already received endless messages about their body, body size, being sexy, etc. They've seen scenes of couples making love or close to it. From sources both negative and positive. It is important for parents to express directly and explicitly what the expectations are for their child's sexual behavior and responsibility.

Again, honesty is paramount. Concerns about sex vary from parent to parent. You may be worried your child will have an unplanned pregnancy, be sexually assaulted, have sex before they are emotionally ready, or be disrespectful to a romantic partner. Whatever your concerns may be, it will be easier for your tween to understand the risks when they have all the information.

When you plan, as you constantly do with the best outcomes in mind, prevention must be in the forefront of your mind. While humans can heal, life is much smoother if wounds and trauma are avoided. An interrupted life is not what you want for your child. Help them be safe by telling them how.

Safety and Unintended Outcome from Having Sex

Beyond unintended pregnancy, health risks exist. Some STIs have lifelong consequences, are passed between partners, and have no cure. One of these is HIV. While it is no longer the automatic death sentence it once was, it hasn't been cured, and a vaccine doesn't exist. Herpes is another, and it causes painful genital blisters and ulcers. Medications are helpful, but there is no cure. HPV, for which there is a vaccine but no cure, can cause cancer in men and women.

In contrast, STIs like chlamydia, syphilis, and gonorrhea are curable with antibiotic treatments. Condoms remain the surest way to prevent contracting STIs, yet they still break and sometimes go unused. As such, they don't always prevent conception, either.

This is factual information your child needs to learn from you, and it need not be used as a scare tactic. You want a well-informed child. Not a frightened one. It's difficult for tweens to imagine their future—having lived for just over one decade. It's impossible to conceptualize the reality of what being twenty-five or thirty-seven or forty-seven will be like. Or even to imagine living with an unwanted disease. Yet, information is powerful.

Another important component of your child's sex education is teaching them how to avoid predators, harassment, and assault. It's not enough to hope it won't happen. It includes being observant, being wise, trusting their gut, and using safety and refusal skills. Both males and females can be victims, so ongoing conversations must happen with both.

The purpose isn't to scare them but to empower them with self-respect, high expectations, and safety as a number one priority. You and

I know that perpetrators' sole function is to lure others to be their prey by gaining their trust. Abusers take emotional and sexual advantage of those who have less power. You are the trusted person to inform, guide, and instruct your child here. They need this training. You will never regret sharing this reality with them.

Chantel Miller's remarkable memoir *Know My Name* tackles her experience being sexually assaulted and what happened to the perpetrator. She recounts her rape and its aftermath, which includes her outrage, confusion, and anger when her assailant was convicted of sexually assaulting her but given only a slap on the wrist by a judge who didn't want to "ruin" the young man's life. She criticizes our culture's tendency to police young women's behavior, expecting them to be the gatekeepers, and failing to teach men to be respectful and responsible. The truth is the only thing that always prevents assaults is for men to not assault.

We have a long way to go as the message about men taking what they want is unfortunately pervasive. With the continuing acceptance of sexism and misogyny, bad behaviors by the morally bankrupt have become normalized and accepted. Why else would men convicted of rape and assault still play in the NFL, known clergy who are proven sexual offenders remain protected and serve in churches, and celebrities and others with power and privilege intimidate and pay off those they've assaulted or impregnated?

When the powerful and wealthy and even the bully next door get to freely live outside the law, it's profoundly vital to teach respect, safety, and personal sexual accountability. We can and must teach our sons to respect women at all times. And demand that the entertainment providers stop promoting misogyny, abuse, and patriarchy. And teach how women and men can protect themselves. We must. While this paragraph sounds harsh, we all know it is true. We must instruct our children differently.

Asking for Consent and Body Boundaries

When is it okay to touch another person? Only when they give permission for us to do so. We can't read anyone's mind or assume we know what they want or think. What has to happen is that we must ask if each particular thing is okay.

- "May I _____?"
- "Is it okay if I _____?"
- "Would you like me to _____?"

It's important to listen to the answer and also pay attention to body language.

If verbal permission is given to touch a woman's breast, but their arms are folded across their chest, the answer is no. Also, permission can never be granted from a drunk or high person. Any no answer is *no*.

Ideally, establishing body boundaries starts at a young age when a child not wanting to be kissed by an aunt or hugged by his grandpa is honored. Then the aunt and grandpa don't do it. This reinforces the child's power over their body. It's not too late to talk about this and do it. For if a child knows how to say *no* within the family, it's easier to apply outside. And when they practice using their voice, it becomes easier and easier to use it.

Leading the Conversation about Sex

Most parents have the best intentions when it comes to talking about sex with their tweens, but they get stuck or tongue-tied when it's time to begin. First, and most important, simply start these conversations as soon as possible so you can gain their respect and trust. Let them know that they are the best person to take care of their body. Stress that it is *their* body, and they only get one, and caring for it matters. They know this from brushing their teeth, bathing, and using sunscreen. You've already set an expectation of personal responsibility.

Second, assume that your child will do the right thing as you converse, and in time, they will come to understand what the right things are. Have confidence rather than doubting. Talk about tricky situations they may find themselves in, and ask, "What would you do if this happened? What might have kept it from happening?" Help them imaginatively solve problems. Use your collaboration skills from

Chapter 3 to guide this discussion and to find ways that you can help—without trying to take over or impose a solution yourself.

You can also directly teach your child specific refusal skills. These include creating an escape plan, developing ways to say no without losing face or making it confrontational. Also, teach them how to handle the emotions or sense of rejection a breakup may induce. You can frame these as problems that need to be trained for, rather than presenting frightening crises. Emotions, as we talked about, should never be ignored.

Although it may be tempting to just tell your child, "Don't have sex until you're married," as with other major life decisions, your tween will ultimately need to figure out for themselves what they want to do and why. But you can be their trusted parent who is there to inform, listen, guide, and support.

Finally, as huge as these issues may seem, remember that you are not starting from square one. You have been teaching them about safety, respect for others, and self-respect their whole lives. Applying these concepts to sex is just another step in lifelong skill-building.

Sexual Preferences, Orientation, and Gender Identification

Up to this point, I have spoken about the importance of having open, honest, and factual conversations with both your daughters and sons. I would be remiss not to point out that sexual identity is a major component of their lives and is not always easily understood.

Often youth are much more knowledgeable than their parents about what it means to be gay (attracted to a same-sex person), transgender (to be a different gender than the biological one at birth), to be gender-nonconforming (to not follow or obey expected gender stereotypes in clothing, hairstyles, roles, etc.), to be bisexual (attracted to both sexes), to be nonbinary (to be someone who does not match up with either the category of male or female), and more. Through a variety of sources, their awareness is higher. And because they are defining their sexual identity themselves, they think about it more than adults. It's possible they have friends grappling with less common sexual identities.

From our perspective, understanding and accepting an identity other than what we envisioned for our child can be a struggle and an adjustment. Or maybe you've seen signs along the way and are not surprised. Either way, it takes time and patience. Keep in mind that no child would choose an alternate sexual identity or lifestyle.

Like everything else about your child, as tweens attempt to figure out their identity, they need parents who accept the reality of their child's sexuality and gender orientation, no matter what. This is one of the most appreciated things you can do for your child. As we know from our discussion of identity in Chapter 1, children don't want to be or feel isolated or ostracized. Fitting in is vital, and continuing to fit in at home and with the extended family is essential no matter what. Being separated into a category with the heading of "something I don't approve of" or "something harmful to others" can damage your child. We do not want to judge them for something they have no control over.

This acceptance is even more crucial if you live in a culture where members of the LGBTQ community are under attack. It gets complicated if your faith base has a negative outlook. And it's thorny if family members openly oppose these orientations. Your loyalty lies with your child no matter what. You know and love your child from the depth of your heart.

Tweens never fail to surprise me. A few years ago, I was chatting with a twelve-year-old when she mentioned her friend, Elliot. After a while I asked, "Is Elliot a boy or a girl?"

"Neither," she told me. "Some days Elliot feels more like a girl, and some days they're more like a boy."

This young lady easily accepted Elliot and their wavering identity. It wasn't a big deal for her, and she used they/them pronouns without even thinking about it. To this day I still don't know Elliot's sex. She summed up her acceptance with this question to me: "Does it really matter?"

When your child reveals their truth about their sexual identity to you—and what they tell you is not what you expect to be true for them—recognize that you have been successful establishing a relationship that is open and encouraging to them. They trust you with their truth.

Please recognize that saying this *aloud* to you takes courage and strength. Consider all that came before and how they might have been overcome with uncertainty, confusion, and even some embarrassment. As they discerned their sexual preference and identity to be different from most of their peers, they may just now be coming to terms with it. Accepting this difference was probably exhausting for them. As well, finding ways to assimilate this internally and socially with peers was likely taxing. Finally, the worry about your response might have been arduous. This was a tremendous journey for your child.

Your response to them must be love, because what you say at this moment in time will be long remembered. It's okay if you are shaken, shocked, or okay. Take a silent moment to deal with your emotions. Then acknowledge your child and your love and commitment to them. You may want to start the conversation with one or all of the following:

- "Thank you for telling me."
- "I appreciate you telling me."
- "I stand with you."
- "You are my precious child."
- "I love you just the way you are."

Whatever your child's sexuality, they are still the person you have loved all these years. Acknowledge their truth to them, and be clear that you love them unconditionally. You won't judge them—because, in fact, there is nothing to judge. And like all the other areas to chat about, this will not be a stand-alone one either.

Sex, Love, and Relationships in Action: Caleb's Story

Let's return to Caleb and his parents, Michelle and Dean, from the start of this chapter. Recall that one benefit of practicing good communication with our children is that we can recognize when we've made a mess of it. Fortunately, we can create an opportunity to try again.

The next morning, instead of rushing around getting ready, Caleb's parents sat down with him to eat breakfast. "We're going to give you a ride to school instead of having you take the bus," Dean explained, "so we can have some time to talk about Grace."

"We're sorry about our abrupt answers to your questions last night," Michelle began. "May I answer your questions about Grace now?"

Caleb nodded. "Do you really think Grace is stupid?"

Mom tapped his arm gently. "No, I don't think Grace is stupid. That was a bad word for me to use. She's really smart, like you."

"So why did you say having a baby was a bad idea?"

"Having a baby when you're college-aged and don't have a job will be difficult. I'm worried about Grace. It's not my place to judge her or her life. What I can do is be supportive."

"So, you think it's okay she had sex?"

Michelle took a deep breath the way she does when she's trying to think of an answer. Caleb waited. "So, do you remember when we spoke about sex in the past, and Dad and I talked about relationships?" Caleb nodded. "It's a very personal and private decision. If Grace and her boyfriend decided they were ready for sex, they might have thought about birth control. Deciding to have sex isn't the same as deciding to have a baby."

"Yeah." Caleb nodded some more. "I know you said that before. That makes sense. But does everybody in college have sex—like you said, Dad?"

Dean coughed. Michelle gave him the side-eye. "I don't know," he said honestly.

"Okay, I'm know I'm not ready. I don't even like anyone enough." Caleb moved a spoonful of cereal into his mouth.

"I hear you." Dean nodded.

Caleb swallowed. "Yeah. This eighth grader on the bus said he sent a girl a dick pic. Why would he do that?"

Michelle nearly slapped her hand over her mouth. "That's a hard question to answer."

Dean shook his head. "I don't know."

"Okay. Hey, I have to bring my extra PE shirt. Good thing you're driving me today," Caleb remarked.

Key Takeaways

The world is huge and made even larger by the media. The messages about sex are pervasive—from clothing, scenes in shows, language, attitude, etc. I urge you not to forget that the impact and influence you have as a parent is greater. Your faith in your child to make good decisions and not take crazy risks is necessary. All the opportunities you've taken to guide and understand your child matter. Having them well prepared for the sexual side of themselves is the best thing you can do. Your words, availability, and understanding make their lives better.

You want to be the person they know they can come and talk to about whatever is happening in their lives. They may keep some aspects of their sexuality a secret, just as you do, but you want to encourage the reality that your door is open, and you will give accurate and honest information.

You can guide your tween effectively by doing your research so that your information is accurate and by being honest, especially about the fact that sex is pleasurable. You can use these conversations to help them clarify what they value in themselves and others and teach safety, self-respect, and respect for others—lessons that can be applied to areas beyond sex and relationships. If your tween talks with you about explorations of sexual orientation and gender identity, remember to be supportive, loving, and nonjudgmental. You've got this!

Your Key Takeaways: Your Turn to Write

Name three things you learned.

1. _____

2. _____

3. _____

Name two awarenesses you'll embrace.

1. _____

2. _____

Name at least one thing you will apply. What will you do differently?

1. _____

So much of what your child needs to learn about sex also has to do with the concept of personal responsibility, which has broad implications in the tween years and beyond.

Chapter 6
Privilege and Responsibility—How to Get Beyond Entitlement

Jennifer and Tom looked defeated sitting in my office. Their sixth grader, Aiden, excelled on his sports teams but was barely making it in the classroom.

"He lacks for nothing," Jennifer lamented. "We take him to baseball and football games. We get him his favorite team jerseys, the latest shoes, and the newest devices. We never miss his games, and we cheer for him. We're proud of the effort he puts forth athletically; he's so talented. But he won't do his schoolwork."

Tom nodded. "He's such a sweet and funny kid, and he's bright—he can tell you the stats of every player on the Dallas Stars and knows the scores from every year the Cowboys have played in the Super Bowl. But he has no interest in school or learning. He does only the exact amount of work necessary to keep his grade above a 69 so he can still play sports, and that's it. We love him. But we can't get him to do anything. If we ever try to talk about what he's learning, he rolls his eyes and says he can't remember. We don't know how to motivate him."

"I think you're right. Aiden's a great kid," I told them sincerely. They were caring parents in a hard position. "When I visit with him, he's respectful and friendly and chatty—until we talk about his grades. Then I see the same thing you see as he stares at the wall. He can't wait to get out of the conversation. The last time we met, I asked him if he worried that he might not be able to play football if his grades got any lower, and he just shrugged. We know from his state tests that he's got a solid academic core, and he's been screened and has no learning disabilities. Tell me more about how it goes at your house."

"We've tried everything!" Jennifer threw her hands in the air. "When we looked at his last report card, we took away his phone and TV. He spent the weekend studying, so we gave them back, and then he quit doing his work again. When his next test grades were low, we grounded him. He studied for his next test, so we let him have friends over again, but then he stopped studying. It's the same pattern—we take things away, he works just hard enough to get them back, and then he goes back to his old ways. It's a constant battle."

"Frankly," Tom glanced at his wife before continuing, "we're not always consistent. He cries when we say we're going to take his phone away. He tells us he can't go to sleep without watching *SportsCenter*. He says he'll lose his friends if he can't hang out with them. He becomes so miserable that it makes us miserable, so we give in."

"What responsibilities does he have at home besides schoolwork?" I asked. "Any chores or household jobs?"

They shake their heads. "We don't want to distract him from school, football, or hockey practice," Tom said.

"If he can pull up his grades, then he can take on more responsibilities," offered Jennifer.

"Hmmm." I tapped my pen on my desk. Unfortunately, I needed to tell these parents that they have caused this problem by entitling their son to unlimited privileges with no strings attached.

Sometimes, as definitely with Tom and Jennifer, your child's issues are rooted in your leadership style and point of view. Accepting this means parents have the power to replace the strategies and mindsets that don't bring out the best in their children.

When Parents Give Too Much

When parents give privileges to tweens that they did not earn, it is often done to avoid conflict and provide ease. Another reason is that when children are emotional and upset, parents feel their pain. An additional reason is the parents' inability to hold the line because they are easily persuaded, and they cave.

All too often we categorize and assume that conflicts are painful, stressful, and problematic. Some of us have a flight response. We would rather avoid the problem because we've accepted that it is safer to do so. It appears, to our mistaken belief system, easier to smooth it over than go through what we erroneously perceive as probable pain. But what happens then is that the issue moves up a notch, simmering below the surface and awaiting its next chance to rear its gnarly head and seek a resolution.

What is true is that disagreements are a normal phenomenon in our shared humanity. They serve to alert us to a problem. They provide opportunities to understand each other and resolve problems. I urge you to shift your perception and view conflicts as beneficial events. And breathe in the fact that clashes are with ideas and preferences, not with people.

Emotions play into every situation. When a child is upset that something unwanted happened, they will have feelings. And that is normal. When their emotions become our emotions, we block our cognitive functioning. It's impossible to act in a way that helps your child in the short and long run when you make decisions based on their emotions.

Please, take a minute to recall what you learned about emotional regulation so you can let your tween own their emotions: you understand their feelings, and you then respond with empathy, calm, and confidence. And please don't doubt your child's capacity to deal with their disappointment. By undercutting and dismissing their abilities, they get the message they are unable to deal with setbacks, as well as their emotions.

Parents often tell me they have trouble following through on decisions they believe were well-founded. One told me, "When my child got in trouble at school last week, I immediately texted her that she wouldn't be attending the high school volleyball game that night as planned. Once home, she cried and pleaded with me about how horrible it would be if she missed it. Her friends would feel let down. They'd have to find another ride. And she went on to guarantee perfect behavior in the future. She went on bargaining to take on a new chore and be nicer to her brother. She was beside herself. I gave in. It was going to be too painful for her. I felt bad for her. And it would also be disastrous for me."

You and I can imagine that this is not the first time this young lady used these tactics to get her way. Because it has worked time and time again, the child knows how to use these manipulative tactics. In spite of the child's ploys, the parents must follow through on their initial decision. Which, in this case, is losing a privilege because of a poor choice.

Not sticking to the plan relegates parents to the cheap seats where the pushovers hang out. Not holding the line now will lead to more intense agony and higher-stakes negative consequences later.

And Aiden is better off learning responsibility and accountability in seventh grade than when he is an adult who loses his job because he didn't learn how to work diligently as a youngster and deal with emotional fallout.

It is easy to acquiesce to avoid the pain of conflict and emotions, as well as to have to live with a leaky line for expectations. Sometimes it feels like saving our child from painful logical consequences is helping them. Sometimes it feels good to be what our child claims is us being the best parent ever, the hero, saving them.

However—and this is a huge however—you are not helping them when you take the conflict-free, emotionally hijacked, or holey boundary road. A major role of parenting is to raise hard-working problem-solvers.

The only way this can happen is if you design your parenting strategies so your child acquires the skills and habits to follow through, take initiative, accept consequences, and understand that privileges follow responsibility. In Aiden's case, his parents struggle to do the difficult job of holding him accountable. This means he is not learning these life lessons.

It's not too late. You love your child enough to do the best thing.

As the parent and the leader, you need to weigh the learning opportunities that present themselves for long-term success. It's necessary to hold tweens accountable and get comfortable with your child's—and your own—discomfort. Strong leadership requires pushing through the temporary pain to keep the big picture in mind. In this case, the big picture is raising a reliable, competent adult who understands that most things in life must be earned.

It's important to remember that the desire to spare our children discomfort comes from love. We want them to be happy, and we are often motivated to give them things to facilitate that. When parents give too much, it's due in part to the deeply ingrained consumerist nature of our society. We don't often directly address this reality, but it can lead to parents confusing material goods with love.

Nice things can't take the place of good habits. Giving our time, presence, and commitment is more valuable than anything we could ever purchase. When it seems like the goal of life is to get the Ray-Bans, the BMW, or the Guccis, we have an acute case of the wants—and our consumerist economy is right there supporting it. We have to stop and remember what we, and our children, actually need. And what is best for them. And the best use of our funds. No fancy new toy can take the place of teaching our child habits of responsibility, and gratitude too. We need to be careful with handing out material goods and privileges that have not been earned just because it makes us feel good in the moment to do so.

In American culture, so much of our identity is tied to the stuff we buy, the house we live in, or the restaurants we go to. Because tweens are searching for their identity, they are easily caught up in the false narrative that what we *have* is who we *are*. Parents need to guide their children to the higher-level idea that our identity comes from our character, our belief system, our sense of purpose and responsibility.

We begin this journey by getting clear about the relationship between privilege and responsibility.

Rethinking the Privilege–Responsibility Connection

When I talk about "privileges" in this chapter, I am referring to benefits and extras that parents give to children because they earned them. They earn them when their schoolwork, hygiene, chores, clean room, respect, manners, and other responsibilities and expectations are accomplished. This includes their character traits and attitudes. When they fall short, it only makes sense that privileges—like screens, having friends over or hanging out with them, going to games or parties—should not be granted.

This is not the basics like food, clothing, shelter, etc. I am not talking about the economic advantages some families might have. Also, this is not punishing or punitive. It's a simple balance of responsibility and privilege.

Indulging children without the required baseline of behavior and performance guarantees problems. It leads to a child with traits no parent had the intention of instilling: they become ungrateful, indolent, and demanding. In addition, children miss an essential and proven life lesson. With time, they become entitled children who want more and more and do less and less. This is the opposite of what you want—a self-starter who is a responsible problem-solver.

Every parent grants privileges differently, but most parents agree that they do not want to raise a child who feels entitled. A child who has been given all that they desire or demand without earning any of it—even if those things have been given out of love—is missing out on learning that they are competent and capable.

Tweens are old enough to understand that what their parents provide for them comes from their parents' economic resources. Parents take on responsibilities so that they can earn the money to purchase the material goods their families need or want. Most tweens have not earned anything yet. They are 100 percent dependent on their parents.

Your child must be taught the connection between the privileges you give them and the responsibilities that make those privileges possible—between rewards and the hard work that produces them. It may seem obvious to us, but it won't be clear to your child unless you teach them. They need us to point out how taking notes in class, reading the chapter, and doing the homework results in high grades, and how practicing their scales leads to them playing a sonata, and how sprucing their room daily keeps it tidy. It's a series of small things and choices that get big results. They need us to tie their privileges to their responsibilities now so that they understand this crucial connection for the rest of their lives.

As your child matures, privileges and responsibilities must be yoked together. Levels of responsibility and privilege should increase and decrease accordingly—that is, the more your tween fulfills their responsibilities, the more privileges they earn. Likewise, if they take on fewer responsibilities or have trouble meeting current expectations, fewer privileges should be given. Ultimately, the motivation and determination to be productive and successful will need to come from your tween.

This all requires a change in how we—and ultimately, our children—view privileges. *Privileges should not be the default setting.* For example, consider the positioning of video games in many homes. When the video game controllers and TV are sitting right there in the den, your tween may think that they should have unfettered access. They may resent you telling them that they can only play when their homework is done or that you will only purchase a game update if they complete their chores successfully for a month.

But those controllers and the console are there because you paid for them with money you earned from fulfilling your responsibilities at your job. The same goes for the gaming system, the TV, each separate game, and the internet service. Your child needs to earn the privilege of using what you paid for.

Instead of allowing free access, this privilege should be tied to responsibility. Maybe your child gets to veg out with their game for thirty minutes after school to unwind—and this is okay for sure. Maybe they get to play until it is bedtime once their homework and chores are done. Maybe they only get access if they have spoken to their social studies teacher about a low grade on a quiz. Maybe they get to play on Saturday if all their grades are above an 84 and they have completed their chores.

None of these expectations are punishments. You are not taking anything away. Instead, you are granting access. You give a privilege because they met a responsibility. You begin with the responsibility and then balance it with the privilege. Making this philosophical shift is one of the most powerful things parents can do to prepare their children to embrace increasing responsibilities they will encounter in adulthood.

The Power of Responsibility

As we discussed in Chapter 4, responsibilities and accountability lead to feeling accomplished. When tweens complete a job, it boosts their confidence. There is a bump in their self-worth meter—it's notched up because they feel good about what they've done. Often, they get a dopamine ping that feels good, too. Their self-image becomes more positive. By doing the right thing, they grow in wisdom, grace, and integrity.

The sense of competence that comes from meeting a responsibility can lead to increased motivation to meet the next one and then create a cycle of proficiency and mastery. Experiencing success can also build resilience and insulate your tween when they inevitably face failures later. It can also lead to such mature habits as delayed gratification, prioritizing study skills, speaking up for oneself, consistency, planning, and avoiding procrastination.

Developing a sense of responsibility means your tween understands that they have the *freedom to choose* whether or not to meet requirements. They see that responsibility is ultimately self-ordained because they are the ones who will live with the consequences. As your child is working to decide who they are, developing a sense of responsibility means choosing what expectations they want to meet and accepting the privileges—and conversely, the consequences—that go with them. You want to participate in building their internal and positive autonomy and independence.

Ultimately, you want your tween to learn to turn off the screen without you prompting them and start on their math homework or do their laundry. You want them to be self-disciplined, process ideas with clarity, and problem-solve independently. Doing the right thing—the responsible thing—leads to a whole host of privileges granted by parents, school, self, or society. Working hard leads not only to simple "rewards" (I don't have to search for my boots because I put them where they belong, or I printed my report last night so I'm all set for school this morning), but it also encompasses intangible benefits like approval, confidence, and acknowledgment. This intrinsic desire to be responsible will carry them on a course with fewer conflicts as they launch into adulthood.

How to Build Strong Responsibility Habits

Habits are built over time. Practices we do consciously at first can become what we do automatically. If we help our children practice being responsible in small things like putting the cap on the toothpaste or pushing their chair in after dinner, it can become second nature and can extend into other areas of their lives.

You are likely already doing this. What is your child already responsible for doing? What additional habits would be useful to them, and how could you instill them? Growing up in a family allows for thousands of learning opportunities.

Chores

Assigning new household tasks to your tween is a straightforward path. You can transform these chores into a rite of passage: "Now that you are eleven, you are ready to be in charge of feeding and walking the dog daily." Give your tween responsibilities that directly impact them, such as emptying the trash in their room or cleaning the shower in their bathroom. You might also consider jobs that involve coordinating with a parent or sibling, like making part of dinner, adding to the grocery list, helping a younger sibling memorize their times tables, or reorganizing the pantry.

As you assign new jobs, make sure you provide the tools and knowledge your child needs to succeed as well as add a time stamp. Remember also that there may be a learning curve that comes with any new skill, and it will take practice before the kitchen is as spotless as when you do it or the dust bunnies are completely eliminated. Your tween may experience discomfort, inconvenience, and frustration that comes with helping around the house. Understanding their emotions helps them, too. Wouldn't we all rather be binge-watching our favorite show, golfing, or sleeping in late? Adulting and adulting prep require training and sacrificing.

Schoolwork

Supporting solid study habits with cause and effect in mind matters. When your tween can see the connection between time and effort spent and the results produced, it can reinforce their commitment. And that means increased motivation to do it next time. As discussed in Chapter 4, your primary role is to designate *when* homework is going to happen, and then make sure your child has a quiet space and the tools they need to do the work. That's the leadership in you.

You can also help your tween become a more independent learner by encouraging them to study in the ways that are most natural for them. Think about which of the three basic learning styles applies to your tween. Are they a reader, a viewer, or a hands-on learner? For example, a reader will do well looking over notes for a test, while a viewer will do better with pictures, videos, or diagrams, and a hands-on learner needs something to manipulate. Breaking up the steps for how a bill becomes a law, as an example, can be learned by reading the chapter and taking notes, or watching videos with step-by-step visuals, or creating a timeline with coordinating colors. Then think about what you can do to support that kind of learning when your child is studying at home.

Finally, teach your tween the habit of planning out their work and help them break it down into sections. As an example, you could ask your child, "What subject assignment will you do first, and how long will that take you? What will you do next, and how long will that take you?" Homework can seem less daunting when your tween can break it into smaller pieces and predict how much time it will need: "Okay, I'll do the eight math problems first, and that will take me eight minutes. Then I'll do my research on John Quincy Adams, and that will take me thirty minutes. Then I'll get online with my science presentation group for forty-five minutes." Planning helps them learn time management and information processing—both crucial life skills.

Small Habits

Small habits, like having your tween make their bed first thing in the morning or put their PJs in the hamper, are another great way to instill self-reliance. They get a visual reward seeing their room look neat and coming home to a made bed at the end of the day. By accomplishing things first thing in the morning, their morning routine gets going.

The goal is for your tween to develop solid personal starting and completion habits—not for you to have to direct, nudge, nag, or boss them. For example, your tween learns about being on time in middle school because there are class periods. They know they need to pack up their things quickly, remember where they are heading, and focus on getting to the next class on time. This skill set translates to being ready and on time for soccer, scouts, and fencing. And, later in life, to work.

Rewarding Good Habits

Often parents ask me if they should pay their children for good grades. I believe they should not. A tween's job is to learn and do well in school, and that motivation needs to be built intrinsically not extrinsically. Notorieties like honor rolls and the National Junior Honor Society reward students with a status that they've earned. Feeling personal pride for a job well done reinforces their dedication to school success.

I'm more interested in celebrating the habits that lead to positive results. For example, if your child gets their homework done or finishes their chores diligently, occasionally you might say, "You stayed focused and followed through." They'll hear you, see that you care, and feel noticed. When looking at their grade portal with them, you can mention that every assignment was handed in on time. This acknowledges an expected habit, but it does not earn a privilege.

The Value of Money

No discussion of privilege and responsibility would be complete without a word about money. It's necessary that they understand the value of money and develop good spending and saving habits.

A great place to start is with basic spending and budgeting. Many tweens have no sense of how much things cost, especially with the advent of plastic and apps. If you were to ask them how much school lunch or a Big Mac cost, would they know? And is it more cost effective to buy the meal, or only what you actually eat? And what about saving for the new Lego set or concert tickets?

You could use an app such as Greenlight or a spreadsheet program to help your tween track how much money they have and what they spend it on. As part of a discussion on how budgeting will work in the future when they are financially independent, they could show you how they spend their money each month. At first, it may surprise them. Is there anything they would like to change about their spending habits? Keeping an open dialogue about money can lead to further insights.

At the grocery store or when buying clothes, it's easy to compare the value of things. Is the larger size cheaper, comparing cost per ounce, than the smaller one? Is the savings of buying the larger size worth it—will it all be used? When I took my own children clothes shopping, I often pulled out two pairs of jeans and asked which they preferred and why. Much of the time, the only difference was the designer label. Then we looked at the difference in price. I told them that if they wanted the more expensive pair, they would have to pay the difference between that and the cheaper pair. Alternatively, I said I would pay $50 for a sweater. If they found one they wanted that was only $35, they could then put the remaining $15 toward another piece of clothing. This practice made the abstract concept of "the value of money" into something concrete: the difference between two different pairs of jeans or getting two sweaters versus one.

In addition to lessons about spending wisely, it's also important to teach your tween to save. Have your child identify a goal, an item that you are not willing to pay for such as a new video game or makeup. Help them work out a plan for saving a certain amount over a set period of time, and brainstorm ways for them to earn the money they need, such as doing odd jobs or waiting for a birthday check from Uncle Bob. This exercise will help them understand that money is not an infinite resource but something they worked for. They may also find they enjoy the things they have to wait and work for more than any instant gratification.

As you begin discussions about budgeting, spending, and saving, your tween will need a chance to practice these lessons. Allowances are a good idea, but be clear about what that money is designated for. Is it just for having fun? Should they put half away for a future car or for college? Are they supposed to pay for their own school lunch? Set clear expectations and help them be responsible for where that money goes rather than just handing them some cash each week, and you will turn the allowance into a real tool for learning.

Some lessons about money are more abstract and will require ongoing discussions. For example, we want our children to value hard work as a means to earn privileges, but there is not an absolute connection between hard work and money earned. Hard work is not always well-paid work, such as the work done by hotel housekeepers, garbage collectors, and stay-at-home parents. Similarly, someone who has a lot of money is not always someone who works hard to get it. It is also true that money is not the only payoff for hard work—other benefits include taking pride in what you do, helping others, or feeling a sense of accomplishment.

Ultimately, any discussion about money can also be a discussion about values. Once, I was in line at the grocery store and heard a very illuminating conversation between a mom and daughter:

"We have to practice expository writing. I picked the prompt about our family values and what makes our family special. I decided what we value is having money," the tween said.

The mom, clearly taken aback by this answer, kept her cool. "Why is having money the most important thing about our family?" she asked.

"It's the thing that makes me feel good. I don't ever have to worry about not having money for lunch, or if I can go to Starbucks. I like that we drive a new car."

"Hmm," the mom replied. "What other things do we value? What other things are important to us as a family?"

After a pause, the girl said, "I'm not sure."

"Well," the mom said, "do you value our family vacations together? Spending time with your friends? Your religious beliefs? Making Saturday breakfast with Dad? Being truthful? Singing in the school choir?" As the mom ticked through her list, the daughter said yes to all the things she mentioned. At the end, the mom said, "Which of those things do you value most?"

"Having money," the daughter replied. "That's still the top thing I value."

The mom squinted at her daughter. "You're right. Money gives us an opportunity to have some nice things, but to me, relationships and character count more. I value how kind you are, how much you love animals, and how generous you are to your brother and sister."

This last remark by the mom was a great idea. Instead of questioning her daughter's values or saying she was disappointed, she gave her daughter a different point of view for her to think about, and in a way that showed how much her mom appreciates her. She turned it around so the daughter could realize all these valuable things have nothing to do with money.

One Other Thing: Gratitude

Children are privy to our convictions and values because we demonstrate them without even thinking. If we are on time, if we say please and thank you, if we speak softly, our children see this and often emulate it.

If we are short on expressing gratitude or appreciation, however, our children will likely also follow suit.

I met a dad who was concerned about his sons' lack of gratitude. He felt they didn't appreciate his hard work and completely lacked gratitude for all that came their way. Simple things like a neighbor bringing over dessert, or his teacher giving him special help after a long absence, or one brother taking the laundry upstairs for the other all went without a response—as if these things were normal or simply expected. When asked, one son shrugged his shoulders and asked if gratitude was really a thing, because those three things were pretty ordinary.

Somehow amid all the things this dad had taught his sons, he had overlooked gratitude. He hadn't taught them, in words or by example, to take a pause to experience and then comment on a kindness or thoughtful gesture, or even the luxury of having a phone. Or to consider the significance or value of the person behind the action. They were unfamiliar with feeling chosen, special, or thankful.

Gratitude is not limited to saying "Thanks." It is about *feeling* appreciative for what has been done or given. The emotion behind gratitude changes the hormones in our brain that make us feel happier, sleep better, exercise more, and strengthen our immune system. Speaking of brain changes, gratitude also nudges the **Prefrontal Cortex** because we are actively thinking about it and putting it into words or actions.

We want tweens to be grateful—to appreciate the people who give the privileges and extras that come their way. Fortunately, helping them develop gratitude is easy. Start by modeling it. Not only will you get the benefits from experiencing gratitude, but your children will see it. You could text your kids or leave notes for them about what they did that made you feel grateful.

- "You were the last one up last night, and you turned off all the lights before you went to bed—I appreciate you doing that."
- "Thank you for packing the baggie of your homemade chocolate chip cookies and leaving it on my bag this morning.

You made me feel special."

You can begin a dinner table routine by letting each person share what happened that they are grateful for.

- "Jackson reached up and got the plates from the cabinet so I could set the table. I'm grateful to him cuz it takes forever to get out the step stool and then put it away. I didn't even have to ask him."
- "I got in the car without my saxophone this morning. I'm grateful to you, Mom, for reminding me to grab it."
- "I'm grateful for my boss giving us the Wednesday before Thanksgiving off."

You can become a "noticer" by observing small things and commenting on them. If you walk by your child's room, and it's clean, say, "I appreciate how you take care of your room." When you see your child's phone in the kitchen being charged well before bedtime, say, "Thanks for being accountable for your phone being in the charger." It's not a big moment, just a few words that will reach their head and heart. Small things add up.

Once, I assigned a mother and daughter who were experiencing lots of conflict the task of journaling to each other. One prompt asked, "What is one thing you are grateful for in the other person?" When they shared their entries, they realized they had qualities the other saw in them they were unaware of. Another prompt was "Name one thing your mom/daughter did that you liked." Again, what they wrote had gone unmentioned and unnoticed. These exercises helped them grow in respect and appreciation for each other.

You may wonder how gratitude fits in with privilege and responsibility. Gratitude shines a spotlight on the good things and people in our lives, and our mental health. We want tweens to feel gratitude for the privileges we give them and for the responsibilities they take on. And for all the things in between. We learn things in small batches, so the more you sprinkle gratitude around, the habit becomes a natural part of thinking and contributes to a positive mindset for your tween and you.

Privilege and Responsibility in Action: Aiden's Story

When Aiden's parents came to see me about their son's lack of motivation, they felt like hopeless failures. But as I talked with them about the connection between responsibility and privilege, reliable ways to build self-discipline, and the value of gratitude, they started feeling encouraged and realized they needed to shift their long-held beliefs. They recognized that their low expectations were what Aiden lived up to. And they recognized it was fueled by their emotional fears of him feeling left out and feeling bad. They were humble, accepting that their belief system and attitude had steered them away from being the leaders their son needed.

That weekend, Tom and Jennifer sat with Aiden. "We need to do some things differently, son," Tom told him. "We want to chat because we've realized some things."

"You just mean I'm in trouble, and you're going to punish me." Aiden picked up a baseball and spun it in his hand. His eyes were on it, not his parents.

"No," Jennifer assured him. "The plan is not to punish you."

He looked up, wary. "So school doesn't matter?"

"Oh, it matters," Jennifer nodded. "And it will matter to *you* more. Doing your homework and chores will be normal. We want you to learn that the bonus things you have and get to do are privileges. You'll be able to earn them."

Aiden's jaw dropped as Tom added, "This might all sound impossible and unfair to you, but in the long run, you're going to become more independent, confident, and in charge of your own life."

Aiden dropped the baseball on the couch and began to cry. "But I'll never be able to do all that! And you can't make me like school, no matter what you do!"

Tom and Jennifer looked at each other, then both reached out to Aiden. "We're going to work through this new plan together. You're going to help us come up with reasonable expectations. And you're right, you might never like learning. But you just might learn that the skills that make you an outstanding athlete will cross over into being a good student."

Aiden wiped his hand across his face and sniffed, but his tears still flowed. "That doesn't sound right. How?"

"You already know how to work hard from hours on the basketball court and baseball field. Doing drills is like homework, and games are like tests. Doesn't that Steph Curry poster on your wall say something about trying hard? What does it mean?"

"It means you are better than you think and to never stop trying. That means a lot to me for sports, but not school. School sucks. It's no fun."

"I like that reminder. And I believe it's for everything—not just sports and school." Jennifer smiled. Aiden did not.

Tom put his hand on Aiden's shoulder. "We're sorry, Aiden. We let you down by not having high standards for you in school all along. We let you slide—we were afraid. We didn't want you to miss out, and we gave in too often. That didn't help you."

"So it's not all my fault?"

"Nope. We all got here together. And we will move forward together." Tom took a long breath. "That means we have to be accountable to each other."

Aiden didn't look convinced, but he was looking at his parents for a change.

"This is what we are thinking and are willing to do. You will earn privileges by doing your chores and keeping your grades up all the time. We'll set the goals together. We won't let you off the hook as we did in the past." Jennifer believed what she said.

"This sounds horrible," Aiden said, standing up then. "My life of fun is over! What privileges are you talking away?"

"By keeping your grades up and doing things at home, you'll earn your phone, screen time, and going to NBA and NHL games," Jennifer went on. "I know it sounds horrible, but it's not, as long as you do the things we set out. You can get a homerun every time because that part is on your shoulders."

By having the gumption to make this huge change, Aiden's parents are on their way to launching a child with valuable life skills and a range of responsible habits.

Key Takeaways

Parents must find the appropriate balance between privilege and responsibility. Meeting responsibilities should confer privileges, rather than privileges being automatic. Sometimes parents can give too much out of a desire to avoid conflict and because they have mistaken consumerism for love, but if they change course, they will see that responsibility builds empowerment, self-esteem, resilience, and a sense of self and confidence in their tween.

To foster this, parents need to set expectations that will teach children that working hard will pay off for a lifetime. This habit development is the key to creating a cycle of success. Educating tweens about money and the value of gratitude will also produce lifelong benefits.

At times you will have to be okay with your child's discomfort. Disappointments will happen, and your child will learn from them. You saw the hard lesson Aiden had to learn after living on the easy-peasy road his parents had provided for too long. As your tween's identity as a responsible person emerges, they will be unfazed making choices in their favor and earning privileges. Successfully mastering their environment is an essential step to adulting well.

Your Key Takeaways: Your Turn to Write

Name three things you learned.

1. _____

2. _____

3. _____

Name two awarenesses you'll embrace.

1. _____

2. _____

Name at least one thing you will apply. What will you do differently?

1. _____

☼✳☆◯☽☾

Teaching responsibility is hard. As parents, we don't always get everything right the first time, and that's okay. It's why second chances are so important.

Chapter 7
Second Chances—the Choice for Better Outcomes

The house was dark when Diego entered after work. He flipped on the light in the family room and was surprised to find Mateo sitting on the couch, holding his baseball mitt. "How was the game, *mijo*?"

"Why do you care?" Mateo's tone was bitter. He kept his eyes turned away from his father. "You didn't even bother to show up like you promised you would."

"I know. I'm sorry." Diego crossed his arms over his chest and leaned against the doorjamb. "I had to work."

"You promised you'd be there!" Matteo punched his baseball mitt. "You told me last night you'd come, and we'd get burgers after. I tried calling and texting to see where you were, but you ignored me. You didn't answer one of them!" He wiped tears from his face and glared at his dad. "After we won, I had to ask Ryan for a ride home because you didn't even bother to pick me up either. I told my coach and the team you were going to be there. I looked so stupid!"

"Look," Diego's voice was loud. "My boss blindsided me. He threw a bunch of work at me that I had to complete before I left. I didn't have a choice."

"You said this morning you'd be there!" Mateo shouted.

"Don't you raise your voice at me!" Shaking his finger at Mateo, he continued, "I just told you, I had to work. A customer needed something yesterday."

"Everyone had a ride home," Mateo seethed. "Everyone had someone there cheering for them. Everyone had someone there that cared about them. Everyone except me." He threw his glove to the floor and left the room, snarling at his dad.

"You are not allowed to talk to me that way. I deserve to be respected. Someday you'll understand what it means to put food on the table and pay for your sports."

Investing in Second Chances

Intuitive and successful leaders recognize that mistakes happen and use them as a springboard for learning. Second chances transpire in families when apologizing, offering a fresh start, and second-tier learning become the go-to responses to conflicts. The value lies in restoring relationships based on curiosity, grounded in understanding, and designed for connecting.

You can relate to these examples of second chances in action. When you sense or know for sure that your tween is lying, without judgment, you can give them a fresh start to tell the truth. When your children argue over something ridiculous, and you react by yelling at them, you can apologize to them. And when they didn't study for a test or sent an evil text, you can gently ask them what they would do differently next time to obtain a better outcome.

Second chances elevate truth over lies, allow for cognitive processing, and hold each person in high esteem. They make us each a little humbler and loving. We get to be our better selves and bring out the best in our children.

Learning to sincerely apologize and make amends puts the focus on people and their feelings rather than on who is right and who is wrong. Likewise, offering tweens the chance to tell the truth instead of defending a lie also builds trust in both directions. When we give second chances to our tween and ask for second chances when we have made mistakes, we strengthen our relationships instead of allowing conflict to fester and drive us apart. The results stand far above punitive measures.

We all know what it's like to look forward to something the way Mateo did. He expected his dad to cheer him on from the stands and go to dinner with him after the game. When Diego broke his promises, Mateo felt abandoned, ignored, and forgotten. You know, when we tell everyone something is going to happen and it doesn't come to fruition, it's embarrassing, and we feel small.

When Diego approached his son, fully aware he had let him down, initially he apologized, but then he became defensive, and that turned into anger. When Mateo stated how he felt, his dad didn't honor Mateo's feelings or understand his perspective. He blamed his boss and did not take any responsibility for what happened. He did not convey any of his regrets to his son and instead accused him of being too immature to understand the burden of financially supporting a family.

Diego's mistake is not only that he missed his son's game and left him stranded. It's also his poor handling of his mistake when he got home and could chat with Mateo. By not humbly apologizing and empathizing, they both suffer, and a more intense conflict ensues.

The culture you create in your family by giving and receiving second chances builds and mends relationships as it grows trust and respect for each other. We get to be our better self and bring out the best in others.

Resolving Conflicts

When I write about conflict, I simply mean any time parents and tweens disagree. Conflict doesn't have to be about a major issue or involve an intense shouting match. A conflict is also when your tween wants to see the new Spider-Man movie and you want to see the new chick flick, or when you and your spouse want to go to the Italian restaurant and your tween wants to get tacos. These are normal conflicts, and we need to be comfortable with them.

We chatted about conflicts in the last chapter. As parents, we are faced with—and work to resolve—conflicts all the time. Like many parent and tween conflicts, the one between Mateo and his dad stems from conflicting expectations.

It's helpful to understand that conflicts are normal and resolvable. In Mateo's case, his dad is not interested in resolving the issue by listening and understanding. What he wants is to be absolved and right. In wanting to be right, he deflects blame and uses anger as a power source. These actions increase the conflict by heightening emotions and widening the gap between their perspectives on what happened. It moves them further away from a place where Diego can acknowledge that he let his son down.

Criticizing, condemning, and complaining get us away from the real issues and prevent us from resolving the conflict. Instead, strong parent leaders actively create a culture of *resolving* conflicts while honoring each other.

When resolving conflicts, the goal is to restore trust and understanding. Apologizing to your child is important because it means you are *asking to get back into a relationship with them.* It focuses on the real issues at play. Here's an example of a parent trying to resolve a conflict rather than make it worse:

Mike is putting away his tween's clean socks when he finds a vape pen in their drawer. He leaves it there, and he's aggravated and disappointed.

When Parker comes home, however, he stays calm. He says, "I have to apologize to you. We agreed I would respect your privacy and not look in your room. Some of your socks got mixed up with mine, so I thought I'd put them away. I found a vape pen in your drawer. I'm sorry I violated your privacy, and I will try hard not to do it again. However, we'd also agreed that you wouldn't use any tobacco products, so I'd like us to have a conversation about that vape pen."

Mike's words to his son about the discovery check off three necessary boxes. First, he has acknowledged and accepted his mistake of failing to meet Parker's expectation of privacy in his room. Second, he has identified where Parker failed to meet the expectations they'd set up about tobacco use. Lastly, he has presented it as a problem the two of them need to solve. Both conflicts involve trust, and Mike has addressed them rather than focusing on his anger and dissatisfaction. Or on his son being wrong or in trouble. He did not get defensive over his action, nor did he attack Parker about his behavior. This approach opens the door for conversation to resolve the conflict.

Rather than setting up conflicts as "I'm right and you are wrong," parents need to see themselves and their tween on the same team—working to resolve the conflict together. Everyone makes mistakes at some point, and parents and tweens will fail each other's expectations many times in their relationship. Apologize where appropriate and give your tween room to voice their story. Tweens want and need to be heard and understood.

Giving and getting second chances also means focusing on the current issue rather than past incidents. Consider this situation:

Stasia's job every evening is to let their dog, Louie, out into the yard for one last chance to do his business and then bring him inside before going to bed. One evening, Stasia forgets to let Louie back in, and, unfortunately, a rainstorm leaves her mom, Elena, with a muddy, wet mess of a dog to clean.

After dealing with the dog, Elena goes up to Stasia's room and yells, "How could you be so irresponsible? It took me twenty minutes to get the mud out of his fur and paws. I can never rely on you to do what you're supposed to do. Last week you didn't take out the trash. You always say how much you love Louie, but when it comes time to take care of him, you leave it to everyone else." She storms away before Stasia can respond.

The next morning, however, after breakfast, Elena sits down with Stasia and says, "I'm sorry I yelled at you last night. I was harsh and unfair. It wasn't a good way to handle the situation. I know you love your dog. We all forget things sometimes. Let's talk about what you can do to remember to bring Louie in, and how we should handle it if you forget again. Will you forgive me?"

Elena recognizes she made a mistake by going off the deep end the night before. She acted like the situation was about a character flaw in Stasia and brought up things unrelated to the current issue. The next morning, she makes the right move by apologizing sincerely and shifting the conversation to working together to resolve the conflict. She is curious about what they can do in the future rather than condemning what Stasia has done in the past. She also models a way for Stasia to apologize for forgetting and then moves on to resolving the issue, which is ultimately about parent-child expectations.

Conflicts can be opportunities for tweens to learn—but only if parents remember to frame them that way.

Elevate Truth over Lies

Parents want their children to learn about the consequences of their actions, so offering them a second chance when they mess up may seem ill-advised. But we also want them to learn how to express regret and understand that it is possible to start over after a mistake. If we don't, they may resort to lying, which can become a very bad habit. And then, once the lying begins, they work furiously to defend their lie. This is a situation we don't want our child to be in, despite the fact that they will lie to us. If they do lie, you can start the process of second chances by giving them a chance to back away from a lie, as Patty does with her son Jake:

Patty, home from work early, is standing in the kitchen tossing the junk fliers in the recycling bin when Jake comes in. "How was your day?" she asks.

Usually, fourteen-year-old Jake raids the fridge and starts wolfing down food as soon as he gets in the door. But this time, he kicks at something on the floor with the toe of his sneaker and mumbles, "Just the usual."

"I got a call today from the school," his mom tells him. "They said you were absent the last period."

"That's not true!" Jake blurts out. His mom listens quietly as he talks faster and faster. "That teacher is always saying kids are absent when they're not. I bet I was getting a drink when he took attendance, even though he saw me come in and said I could go get some water. That teacher is so dumb. I mean, where else would I be? Of course I was there!"

Patty raises her eyebrow and says again, "I got a call today from the school. They said you weren't present for the last period." She clears her throat. "Do you want to start over with your response? We'll consider it your first answer."

Jake looks up at the ceiling for a moment. Then he nods. "Anuj and Dylan and I skipped last period because it was a pep rally. They're so loud, and it's not like we're learning anything. We just walked out the back door after PE and went to Taco Bell. But then we didn't even get anything because we were so scared we were going to get caught. We hate pep rallies. None of us do sports, and we feel stupid because it's all about how great all the athletes are. But we shouldn't have left school. I'm sorry."

His mom says, "Thanks for telling me the truth. I know it wasn't easy. What should we do now?" By saying this, she leaves the consequences for Jake to decide. And that includes what to do next time there is a pep rally.

By giving Jake a chance to tell the truth after he lied, his mom gave him a powerful lesson. First, she showed she respected him enough to give him a chance to reset—to reconsider his lie. Second, she listened to him explain his motivation. And finally, she empathized with the strength it took him to admit the truth.

Jake came away with the knowledge that his mom did not want him to suffer through an extended lie. His mom remained calm and patient rather than yelling or threatening, suggesting that she valued their relationship and cared about his experience. It didn't mean he was off the hook for bad choices, but it gave him a chance to see that his poor choices—skipping school and then lying—were not irretrievable. And that his mom was on his side.

Remember what you learned in Chapter 1 about impulsive behavior and their **Immature Prefrontal Cortex.** Your child will make mistakes that can't be explained. Their processing and evaluating centers are not mature. They will take risks without thinking of the outcomes or considering all the possibilities now and down the line. This is why they need your help getting out of the situations they create. It's vital to understand they are not doing unexplainable things intentionally.

Avoid putting your child in a position where they feel compelled to dig in and defend their lie because that gets you further away from addressing the real issues. Instead, make it clear that you want to help them tell the truth, wherever it leads. Offer them a fresh start so they can see that fresh starts are both possible and beneficial.

The moment when a parent extends trust, even when a child has breached it, can be profound. Your child can then start repairing that breach with honesty. You can then honor that honesty, and the trust between you and your tween can become even stronger.

It could have just as easily gone this way.

"I know you're lying!"

"Why don't you trust me?"

"I spoke with the attendance clerk. She wouldn't lie.

"'Mom, she had the wrong kid. I was at the assembly; you can ask Anju and Dylan. Call them."

"Why won't you just tell the truth? You know you are guilty!"

"You just want me to be in trouble. You never believe me."

Second-Tier Learning

Giving second chances means accepting that we all make mistakes and that those mistakes do not have to define us. In school, much of children's success is measured by their grades. However, they are also engaged in what I call second-tier learning: the learning that comes after their grade is posted. This is valuable because learning is linear.

For example, on a multiple-choice science test about the moon, a student picked the answer "A: Waning" because they knew the answer began with a "W" and "Waning" was the first option they saw. And then it was the only answer they considered. And they confidently circled A and confidently moved on to the next question.

When they got the test back, they saw that the correct answer was "D: Waxing." This is what they learned: read through all the choices before deciding which one is correct. Don't jump to conclusions. And don't be in a hurry. After all, the test wasn't a timed test. These valuable lessons were not recorded anywhere. But the lessons will resonate with the student as test-taking strategies for a long time to come.

In other words, learning isn't just about getting the right answer the first time. It is also about learning *how to learn better* and understanding that learning is *an ongoing process*. We can always keep adding to our skill sets and to our knowledge.

As parents, we are continuous learners because our children's needs are always changing, especially as they become tweens. A willingness to learn more, to move beyond what we already know and do, is essential. It is part of why you are reading this book! The same approach is important when it comes to making mistakes in the parent-child relationship—for both parents and children.

When either a parent or a child makes a mistake, when they fail to meet an expectation and set up a conflict, they violate trust. They drive a wedge between themself and the other person. Second chances give parents and tweens—or both, because often both parties are making mistakes at the same time—to repair the damage. Second chances say, "I don't want you to be mad at me for the rest of your life. I don't want you to hold this against me today or forever. I want you to trust me again."

In managing conflicts, strong parent leaders are willing to be vulnerable and to be honest about a tough situation. They are able to say, "This is a hard thing to talk about, but I don't want it to drive a wedge between us."

In second-tier learning at school, students learn from their mistakes on tests. In second-tier learning in relationships, each person learns from the mistakes made with each other. And at home, they get to learn how to do a chore better, manage their time, and prioritize.

This kind of learning can be applied to almost any conflict, and it can greatly reduce unneeded strife. We all have moments when we are tempted to react to our child's poor choices with chunks of unkind words and unwanted emotion, but that reaction is never the best option. Consider this scenario:

One night, Ben is jolted out of sleep by a noise. He looks at his clock: 3:00 a.m. Bleary-eyed, he makes his way to the kitchen where his tween, Leah, is laughing at something on her phone—the phone that is supposed to be sitting unused on the counter after 8:00 every night.

"What are you doing on that phone?" he hisses, trying to keep his anger quiet so no one else wakes up. "Hand over that thing down right now. Why do you think you have the right to wake everyone up?"

Leah, looking stricken, gives her dad the phone and whispers, "I'm sorry, I was just—"

"Have you been lying to us all this time about not using your phone after curfew?" he interrupts.

"No!" Leah says loudly. "Why do you always think the worst?"

Ben points an accusing finger. "You've just lost phone privileges for six months!" he barks.

"You're so unfair!" Leah shouts.

Just then, the dog starts to bark, another kid starts calling from their bedroom, and Ben's wife comes into the kitchen, puzzled.

Clearly, this tween has made a mistake. She has failed to follow the phone-use rules, not to mention being inconsiderate, waking people up in the middle of the night. However, Ben ignited the conflict by leaving his daughter no way to respond effectively. Here is another way the situation could have gone:

One night, Ben is jolted out of sleep by a noise. He looks at his clock: 3:00 a.m. Bleary-eyed, he makes his way to the kitchen where his tween, Leah, is laughing at something on her phone—the phone that is supposed to be sitting unused and charging on the counter after 8:00 every night.

"Please give me the phone and go to bed. We will talk about this in the morning," he says.

Leah hands him the phone, and they return to their rooms to get what little sleep they have left to get.

The next evening, Ben and Leah sit down to talk. "We had our sleep interrupted last night, right? Help me understand why you were on your phone at 3:00 in the morning."

"I woke up and remembered I hadn't studied for my social studies test," Leah says, "and then I couldn't even remember what I was supposed to have studied. I ran downstairs to text Shaleena because she gets to sleep with her phone on. She texted me back and said, 'What are you talking about? There's no test tomorrow.' And then I realized I must have dreamed it, so I texted her back, and we were laughing about it. That's when you came in. You can see the whole conversation on my phone. I'm really sorry I woke you up."

By delaying the discussion, they were rested and calm. His goal was to understand his daughter's position. This point needs to be well taken, for the dad wanted to know her story. He knew she didn't usually do anything like this. As such, he didn't presume or assume anything, nor did he set out to prove her wrong or guilty.

Here's one more possibility, this time with Leah's actions needing a firmer response:

The next evening, Ben and Leah sit down to talk. "Why did you make the choice to break the rules last night?" he asks.

"It's a stupid rule!" Leah answers, crossing her arms. "All my friends get to keep their phones at night!"

"If you want to discuss the rule and why we have it," Ben says, "or even if we should change the rule, we can do that, but first we need to talk about last night. Tell me, do you often use your phone in the middle of the night?"

"I mean not often, but sometimes. You just don't wake up, usually."

"I see. And why last night?"

"I couldn't sleep, and I wanted to see if Shaleena could help me with something."

"You see, Leah, I want to trust you. I want us to trust each other. What can we do to restore that?"

In this version, Leah may still lose phone privileges or face another consequence, but she would do so in the context of her dad wanting to trust her. She has the opportunity for a re-do to show she is trustworthy.

As leaders, parents hold the keys to resolving family conflicts. The growth in learning from mistakes in these ways is so much more meaningful than what comes from feeling guilt or shame. What your child takes away is monumental. It is incumbent on the parent to create a culture that supports this learning with collaborative problem-solving and moves them forward with an intact, strong relationship. Just as a test grade isn't the end or even the most important part of learning, the mistakes you and your child make are not the end of your relationship. They are opportunities to mend and grow together.

The Culture of Curiosity

When you give your tween second chances, you eliminate the question-intimidate-demand model. You focus not on getting information but rather on curious care and interest in your child. It lets us wonder about them and their story, and marvel at their strengths and growth.

The question-intimidate-demand model involves asking a rapid-fire series of questions in an intimidating way that demands our child admit they're wrong or justify their behavior. Parents' size, power, and position cause children to freak out, partly because they often already know they did something wrong. And also because they dread what will happen next. When we demand answers and start from a position of accusation and blame, they are put on the defensive. It's impossible for them to see us as a caring ally who will support them. They see that we and they are on opposing sides.

This prosecutorial mindset will not resolve the conflict. It morphs into an even bigger conflict that can send your tween into a flight-fight-freeze response. This happens when your child feels unsafe and unprotected, knowing full well there is nothing they could possibly say that would satisfy you. You do not want to put your child in this situation. They need to feel you have their back, no matter what they might or might not have done. You want a culture of teamwork where you work together: you're on the same side.

You are resorting to the question-intimidate-demand model when you yell at your child: "I know you stole my credit card from my wallet! You used it to buy that video game and ordered candy on Amazon!"

In this situation, your child knows they are wrong. It's likely they feel embarrassed, guilty, and ashamed. And jittery and anxious because they were yelled at. Even if they confess to the theft, how will the chaos of everyone's emotions be assuaged?

To keep the problem to one (remember, emotional upheavals add an additional problem to be solved), be interested and curious about what happened. When your child makes a choice that you see as a mistake, ask them to walk you through their decision-making. Don't be the prosecutor and judge, seeing everything in terms of offenses and guilt. Your goal is to get information. Move from the position of the moral police and become an inquisitive and caring parent. If you approach a conflict with an honest desire to understand what happened, your child won't see the conversation as a battleground where there will be a winner and loser. It is a conversation about information, and information is neutral.

Approaching your child with the desire to help them solve a problem—instead of looking to assign guilt or blame—is an extraordinary mindset for parents to take. It gives your child a platform to explain without fear what happened. It provides you with a stance of valuing the relationship above the conflict. You can build this culture, this mindset. You can make it a rule to live by.

To see how this works, let's say you text your child that you are outside the school to pick them up. You can see they have read the text, but they don't respond. They don't come out for thirty minutes. When they finally come out to the car, you could say, "Why did you ignore me when I told you I was here? Don't you care that I waited for thirty minutes when I had other things to do?" This questioning assumes they made the choice of ignoring you and blames them for wasting your time.

Instead, you could respond with curiosity and neutrality and acknowledge their usual punctuality, like in this example: "Are you okay? I want to understand what happened between when I texted you and now. You usually respond and come right out." When you choose this approach, your concern is them. Then you become privy to the story—maybe they were having a really fascinating talk with their English teacher about a book, or having a big fight with their best friend, or helping a classmate who was in crisis. We all want to know the stories of our children's lives when they are away from us.

This doesn't mean you forego accountability. You can begin this part of the conversation with, "I appreciate you explaining what happened and I understand why. Let's talk about responding to my text and reducing the wait time. What could you do differently next time to honor both of us?" The thing I love about this kind of engagement is that the ideas come from your child. It also opens the door to apologizing and understanding your position.

This approach works well for recognizing a wrong, opting for better choices in the future, and renewing our commitment to each other. Whether it's your tween eating the donut you were saving, leaving the toilet seat lid up, or not returning your phone charger. You can ask for information so you can focus on the problem—the missing donut, the open lid, the missing charger—instead of labeling your child as the problem. This is how you give your child a second chance to address the situation and fix the problem. When it comes to conflict, we want to give our tween the opportunity to take responsibility for solving it.

When we use the question-intimidate-demand model, we create a battlefield of opposing forces. But the last thing you want is to make your child feel like your enemy. If this happens, your child may not want to come to you when they make mistakes in the future. You definitely do want your tweens to come to you when they make mistakes:

Ruby approaches her dad, Isaiah, as he is working at the dining room table. She says quietly, "You're going to get an email from my teacher telling you I said the s-word in class today."

Isaiah looks up from his laptop. He responds with curiosity, "And did you say the s-word in class?"

"Yes," Ruby says. "I got frustrated when I was doing classwork."

"Please, take a seat," Isaiah says. Once she has sat down, he goes on,

"I have trouble with those kinds of words, too. You're going to get frustrated many more times at school and in life, right? What do you think will happen if you keep using those words?"

Ruby thinks for a minute. "I'll get detention, and you'll be pretty disappointed with me. And I'll be mad at myself."

He nods. "That sounds about right. So, what could you do differently next time?"

"Next time I get frustrated, I could tap my pencil really hard. Or...take a deep breath like mom does when we aggravate her. Or...I could come up with another word to say that's okay, like 'sassafras.'" She pauses. "What do you do when you get frustrated at work? I hardly ever hear you swear."

Instead of turning into an argument about swear words, free speech, or respecting one's elders, this exchange became an opportunity for parental vulnerability, problem-solving and even collaboration. Children can come up with extraordinary insights and ideas when we approach them open-mindedly rather than with condemnation.

How to Apologize

A sincere, full apology hits the reset button on a relationship. Parents should always apologize when they have made mistakes, because it reestablishes a positive relationship with their child, rebuilds trust and respect, and reaffirms love. When you apologize, you are asking to bring your relationship back to where it was before the mistake—to the status quo of respect and understanding. You are asking to erase the hurt and move forward together.

The Five Parts of an Apology

Clear communication skills are essential to second chances, especially in apologies. There are five key components to every apology:

1. Begin with "I am sorry for..." and then make a clear statement describing your mistake as specifically as you can. Include what effect your mistake had on the other person, such as "my actions made you feel isolated and unvalued."

145

2. Say how you feel about what you did. Use words that indicate your remorse, like "I feel bad," "I regret," or "I feel awful."

3. State clearly that the mistake was your fault. When you take ownership, you need to directly admit you were wrong and made a poor choice. It takes humility and vulnerability to apologize!

4. Ask the person to forgive you. You are asking for you and your mistake to be pardoned—for them to let go of the injustice of what you have done. This step is huge: it is hard to ask for redemption.

5. Finally, make amends. Find a way as best you can to return to what was lost and start fresh. Promise to try your best not to make the mistake again—give a personal guarantee of your integrity. This effort extends a sense of value and worth to the other person whom you injured.

Notice that an apology directly addresses the feelings and emotions of both the person who made the mistake *and* the person affected by it. Apologies need to get into the emotions triggered by the mistake so you can deal with them and move on. Notice also that apologies deal with ownership and responsibility, concepts we have explored in earlier chapters.

Teaching Your Child to Apologize

As parent leaders, we set the standard for how we want our children to behave, so the best way to teach your tween about apologizing is to model it for them. Our children are always watching and observing us. They look at what we do and listen to what we say. Our example looms in their lives more than any other—even when it feels like our tweens would rather talk to anyone but us.

If we tell them not to gossip, but then they see us dishing dirt with one neighbor about another neighbor, we are actually showing them it's okay to talk about someone behind their back. On the other hand, if we talk about the importance of helping others, and then we take them with us to volunteer at the food bank once a month, our message matches our words.

Additionally, children observe and decode our unspoken language. As they watch us pull into the driveway, get out of the car, and walk to the door, they read the signals and ascertain our mood and feelings. Say you got cut off on the freeway coming home and missed your exit, adding ten minutes to your commute. Your foot slams on the brakes in the driveway. Your hand slams the car door closed. Each foot slams into the ground. Finally, you pull open the door with a bright-red face. All those paying attention know something upsetting has happened. This is not all they learn. They learn that physically expressing frustration, annoyance, resentment, aggravation, and anger is the way to do it. The next time your child slams the door when they are mad, you'll understand that you taught them that.

When and how we apologize will also become a model for our child. Each time we apologize, we are developing a practice and building a healing habit. We, therefore, need to be comfortable and vulnerable identifying our mistakes, clearly apologizing, and using body language to communicate our sincerity.

For example, imagine Jillian has stormed into her son Corey's room as he is hanging out with a friend and loudly scolds him for the minor offense of not hanging up his jacket. Later, she asks if they can talk. She turns her body toward Corey and looks him in the eye as she says, "I'm so sorry, Corey. I was wrong to yell at you. It was even worse because I did it in front of your friend. I shouldn't have yelled at you at all. I was upset about something else. I overreacted emotionally and I took it out on you. I will do my best not to do that again. Can you forgive me? Will you give me another chance to be a better mom to you?"

When we humble ourselves to speak honestly about our mistakes, we empower our children to do the same. They learn from our example how to interact effectively with other people. They see the value of getting and giving second chances.

In addition to modeling, we can explicitly instruct our tweens on how to apologize. It's easy to apply the five steps above to an easy example such as not tightening the lid on the mayonnaise jar and the next user takes it out of the fridge, and it falls to the floor and breaks.

The section above on the five parts of an apology serves as a guide through the steps. Practicing when it doesn't count is a wonderful way to learn.

A Non-Apology: All Apologies Are Not Equal

Sometimes we believe we are apologizing when we are really giving a "non-apology." Non-apologies actually do more damage than not apologizing at all. They don't solve the problem or fix the relationship. The non-apologizer makes it sound like the other person is the problem, not them. This is gaslighting. The gaslighter puts the blame on you and your interpretation and refuses to take ownership or show remorse for their poor behavior. There is an implication that one who was wronged is overreacting. Their purpose is to absolve themselves of any wrongdoing and cast the blame elsewhere by manipulation.

A few examples:

> **"I'm sorry you feel that way."** This statement puts the blame on the other person's feelings and reactions, not on what you did. It says the other person is the problem: it's dismissive, invalidates the other's feelings, and is condescending.

> **"I'm sorry you were offended."** This language makes the other person the problem for being offended, not you for doing or saying something offensive. It communicates that you wish they didn't have the reaction they had, not that you wish you had done something differently.

> **"It was a mistake that couldn't be avoided."** There is no personal accountability in this statement. There's no making amends, no demonstration of understanding, and no promise not to repeat the mistake.

> **"It's too bad it didn't work out."** This language provides no accountability, no clear statement of what the mistake was, and no resolution.

Second Chances in Action: Mateo's Story

When we think about Mateo and his dad, Diego, from the beginning of the chapter, it's clear that Diego needs another chance to make things right with his son. Here's how that conversation went.

Diego knocked on his son's closed door and asked, "May I come in?"

"I guess," Mateo replied in a low, hurt voice.

Diego entered the room and sat across from Mateo, who was slouching on his bed tossing a baseball in the air. "May I start over? I want to express what I should have said from the start."

"Whatever."

Diego began by understanding his son's feelings and stating the ways he'd failed him. "You must have been so frustrated with me. I didn't show up to be your biggest fan in the stands today, I didn't answer your calls or texts, and I wasn't there to take you to dinner. You had to ask for a ride, after you'd told people I was going to be there, and we were going out for burgers after. I'm sorry I did those things. I'm sorry I let you down."

"Yeah, it was my best game," Mateo smirked. "I hit a homer and a triple, and I was part of a double play as the shortstop. And we beat the Titans."

"That's great. I'm proud of you."

"But *you* weren't there to *see* it or me."

Diego nodded. "You're right. I blew it. I would have loved seeing you do all those things. I'm really frustrated I missed out. And I understand why my not being there to cheer you on was especially disappointing. You felt all alone on a big afternoon. It took the shine off your great game, right?" Diego tried to name his feelings and his son's.

"Yeah," Mateo answered.

"I'm sorry I disappointed you and made you angry." Diego validated his son's emotions.

"What happened? Why weren't you there?"

Diego shared the information calmly. There was no shouting or getting defensive. "My boss stopped me in the hall late in the day. He said I hadn't submitted a bid that was due yesterday, and I had to send it before the close of business. It was my fault. I messed up—I thought the bid was due tomorrow. It was my mistake, and I had to fix it. I turned off my phone to avoid distractions so I could make it to your game. It was 6:15 by the time I sent the bid. I missed your entire game. I knew I let you down. I broke my promise to you."

"Couldn't you have just told your boss you'd do it early tomorrow?"

Diego shook his head. He wanted to be as transparent as possible. "I wish I could have told the VP that. He was agitated because it was overdue, and the company needed to get the contract. I also wish I had left my phone on. I should have texted you and explained what was going on, and I should have made sure you had a ride home. I'm sorry, son."

"Me too," said Mateo.

"I didn't honor my promise. I made you feel like I didn't value you." Diego got to the emotional heartbeat of their conflict. "I promise I'll do a better job in the future. I want to try to make it up to you. Will you forgive me? And will you give me another chance to be a better dad to you?"

As they sat in silence Mateo softened as he realized his dad had wanted to be at the game. He hadn't forgotten it or thought it didn't matter. "I forgive you, Dad."

"Thank you. I'd hoped you would. I knew this was hurtful."

"And if you want to make it up to me now, we can play chess, but you only get to play with one knight," Mateo grinned.

"Absolutely." Diego smiled back. "I still might beat you, though."

"Ha! You wish." Mateo scrambled to his feet to get the game.

After the chess game, Diego checked in again to ensure all was well by saying, "We're good, son?"

Mateo's decision to forgive his father was one that will benefit him, too. Holding a grudge is exhausting. It's much more freeing, as you know, to let the anger go, though it's not always easy to do so. Thanks to Diego taking full responsibility and offering a sincere apology, they could both move on. The chance to make amends gives parents and tweens a chance to mend and reconnect instead of staying in a state of anger and resentment.

Key Takeaways

Giving and getting second chances in your relationship with your tween benefits everyone. It is ultimately a way of saying to your tween that your relationship with them matters more than any mistake either of you could make.

When you apologize to your tween, you are taking ownership of what you've done, and you communicate that you value them more than being right. Similarly, teaching them to apologize effectively gives them a path back to their relationship with you.

Second chances also let your child tell you the truth and learn from their mistakes. It supports the reality that as they get older, you will be there as a resource when they face challenges or have questions.

You can help them understand those situations when lying seems like a better or safer option than the truth, and let them know you are on the same side. You will help them tell the truth.

Your Key Takeaways: Your Turn to Write

Name three things you learned.

1. _____

2. _____

3. _____

Name two awarenesses you'll embrace.

1. _____

2. _____

Name at least one thing you will apply. What will you do differently?

1. _____

When we connect with our children honestly and show that we value our relationship with them, they feel secure and loved.

Chapter 8
After the Divorce Comes Co-Parenting

Kiana is a talented pianist whose parents were recently divorced. She practices with great dedication two hours a day, either on the grand piano at her mother's house or on the keyboard at her dad's apartment. She never needs to be nudged to practice, as she loves playing, and in fact studies at a conservatory. Both her mom, Kim, and dad, Darrin, do all they can to support her interest and talent, and in general, they are on good terms.

Kiana has a lesson every Tuesday afternoon from 4:00 to 6:00. Darrin always picks her up and takes her to dinner before dropping her off at Kim's.

One Tuesday, Kim received a call at noon from the school. Kiana was not feeling well and needed to go home. The doctor diagnosed Kiana with a sinus infection. By the time they finished with the doctor, picked up the antibiotic at the pharmacy, got settled at home, and called the conservatory, it was dinnertime. Kim began cooking and forgot all about letting her ex-husband know what had happened. And so did Kiana.

Darrin pulled up in front of the conservatory a little before six, as usual. He was looking forward to dinner with his daughter at the Mediterranean place they both love. Kiana was usually outside to meet him by 6:05, but by 6:15 she still hadn't shown up. A little worried, he texted Kim to let her know and then parked the car. Kim didn't hear the text alert.

The conservatory building intimidated Darrin, with everyone looking serious and the hallways so formal. At the main desk, he said he was there to pick up his daughter. "She's usually done at 6:00, so I wanted to see if she'd been delayed. She hasn't come out yet."

The man at the desk checked the computer and said, in a tone suggesting Darrin should have already known, "She did not attend today due to illness."

Darrin felt stupid not knowing his own daughter was sick. He mumbled a thank you and headed outside. He was afraid, thinking maybe it was so serious that Kim didn't have time to call him. He called his ex.

When Kim saw Darrin's name, her stomach sunk. She knew she had messed up. She picked up, and before she had a chance to say anything, Darrin started talking in a brisk, concerned voice. "So, I just walked out of the conservatory. Is Kiana okay?"

"Yes, yes—another sinus infection." Kim tried to sound casual to hide her guilt. "I forgot to call you. Things were hectic. I had to leave work—"

"Do you know how worried I was? First, she isn't where she's supposed to be, and then they say she's sick, and I'm thinking she must be in the hospital, because I haven't heard from you!"

"I was busy taking care of our daughter!" Kim responded to Darrin's indignation, adding some heat of her own.

"Which I could have helped with if you had told me. You know I'm done early on Tuesdays."

"Do you have any idea how hectic today has been?"

"You already said that. Every time, you make it about how busy you are instead of how you like to keep me in the dark."

"You have no idea what my life is like—"

"Don't start. I'm going to FaceTime Kiana."

"Don't do it now. I think she's asleep."

"Then she won't pick up. But I want her to know I'm thinking about her. Just because I'm not there to take care of her—"

"Fine. Whatever. Goodbye." Kim stabbed at the end button on her phone.

The next Tuesday morning, Kim's phone beeped as she took Kiana to school. She asked Kiana to read it to her.

"It's Dad. It says, 'Will Kiana *actually* be at her piano lesson tonight? I'm asking now because I know your day might get too *hectic* to send me any updates.'" Kiana sighed. "I thought you said you two weren't going to be mean to each other anymore."

Does conflict have to be the default when you are co-parenting?

Establishing Shared Goals

Kim and Darrin are on the same page with their love for and commitment to their daughter. However, communication, logistics, and emotional challenges derail their co-parenting success from time to time. In this instance, it's the lack of empathy and thoughtfulness that prevailed.

Kiana scolded and questioned her mom, reminding her that she and her dad were going to treat each other with respect. Kiana, like all kids whose parents are divorced, wants everyone to get along. She doesn't want to be in the middle of her parents' fights, let alone the subject of them. While it wasn't her dad's intention to draw her into this, what is true is that the more parental conflicts Kiana witnesses, the more harmful it is for her.

Although you and your tween's other parent ended your relationship as married partners, you will be connected forever through your children in most cases. The goal of co-parenting is simple, though not always easy to accomplish: finding common ground and full respect with an ex-spouse or partner so you can each provide a stable, nurturing, and emotionally healthy environment with continuity for your child.

The Breakup

The end of a marriage or a split with a significant other is a sad and major life-altering event for children and their parents. Through the physical, social, and emotional transitions, children require support, patience, and understanding from their parents. This is an extraordinarily challenging time for parents who are dealing with their own sense of loss and the unfamiliar, too. Despite their own strong feelings, parents need to be 100 percent present for their children. They are not equipped to deal with their emotions and shaken foundation alone. Both parents need to help them adjust.

Social challenges cause discomfort, too. After a separation or divorce, you may feel isolated missing out on the annual Fourth of July barbecue because the friends who host it invite your ex, not you. You may feel self-conscious attending the yearly school gala fundraiser as a single person. Similarly, your tween may feel awkward at school, where everyone seems to know their business. They may face a new morning routine where they don't see their friends in the carpool or on the bus. Their concerns about fitting in with their friends are high. Both you and your child face adjusting to new roles and identities in terms of belonging.

There are also financial changes. Now that two households need to be maintained, the income and expenses columns in your budget likely look different. You might be tightening your belt for the foreseeable future. Your tween may have to hear the phrase "I wish we had money for that right now" more often than they had before or more often than you'd like to say it. Maybe those extra dollars normally in their Greenlight account are fewer. For parents, the division of who pays for health insurance, co-payments, summer camps, school fees, sports leagues, field trips, clothing, and more can be upsetting. If money issues contributed to the split, this can be an area of unfortunately continued strife unless you agree to not let it be.

Although life changes in a divorce, you get to hold on to your core values, beliefs, and mission. These are the things that define you. They make you *you*, and no one and no circumstances can rob you of them.

You are still you—and you get to be yourself now more than ever. Some parents I work with find it refreshing to no longer be identified as one-half of a couple; for others, the change in identity stings. Most importantly, your identity as a parent has not changed, your child has not changed, and your relationship remains as meaningful to both of you as it always was.

Your principles and beliefs are your center of gravity. Rely on them to work through your transition and help your child to do so as well. Remember that your child will especially need you during this time. Regardless of the pain or challenges you may be experiencing, you will want to make this period as easy as you can for your child—and that goal may in fact help you work through your own feelings.

Your Child's Continuity in the Midst of Change

Of utmost importance to children is their relationship with their parents. Even if it doesn't seem that way, they want to know their parents will be there no matter what. This sense of belonging is very important to all tweens, and even more so during the transition period around a divorce. When their daily structure changes, and they suddenly live in two different homes, their sense of security and safety can be shaken. One parent now lives in a new place—a place that is likely unfamiliar and feels weird. We need to be open and talk about the reality and assure them of our commitment to them by providing consistency. All things you've done to support your bond being strong and fun and honest and energetic need to continue.

Routines matter, so keep your daily structure as similar as possible to before the breakup. Maintain family traditions, such as Sunday pancake breakfasts or Friday movie nights. Expectations, rules, and boundaries should also stay the same to promote continuity. You can assign the same chores, maintain the same bedtime, expect the same amount of studying, and so on. While you might be tempted to make things easier for your child by lessening expectations, this will not be helpful nor beneficial in the short and long term.

Another way to create consistency is to continue to prioritize dinnertime together. Just as before, focus on asking your tween open-ended questions and listening to their answers with curiosity. Talk about how a problem was solved, what's coming up, and the best and worst part of their day. The value of special time gathering around the dinner table is that it prioritizes you as family.

Empathy

Just as parents experience many difficult feelings during and after a breakup, so do tweens. These emotions can cover a broad range, from sadness, loneliness, and a sense of being ignored to uncertainty, confusion, worry, overwhelm, and anxiety. They may also feel anger, disappointment, and even hatred toward their parents.

One of the best things you can do for your child is to recognize and acknowledge what they are feeling. (For a refresher on identifying emotions and speaking to your child with empathy, refer to Chapter 2.) Validating these emotions is important, even when it feels difficult or exhausting for you personally, and even if you are the source of their discomfort—if the divorce was your idea, for instance. Avoid diminishing or dismissing what your child is feeling. Don't try to smooth things over. Let them express how they feel because those feelings are real, and talking about them can be a true relief for your tween.

If your child is *not* talking about their feelings, you can carefully observe their nonverbal communication/body language for additional insight. You can also note what they *are* talking to you about and notice their tone of voice, level of engagement, and attitude. Using your listening skills will help make it clear that you are there to understand and empathize with what they are feeling, no matter how messy those emotions are.

One complicating factor is that tweens often feel at fault or responsible for their parents' breakup. They may think, *If only I hadn't failed that class/been sick for so long/lied that time.* We can watch for these feelings and reassure them that it is not their fault. Use statements spoken kindly like this one: "There is nothing you did or did not do that could have prevented it from happening." We must assuage their discomfort by reminding them their actions had no part in the decision to end the marriage.

It is important that our children feel seen, heard, and understood. As we validate their feelings without defending ourselves or blaming someone else, especially our ex-partner, we can move forward together. We can help them recognize that this is how our family is now. We can't change what has happened, but with empathy, we can manage our new lives.

Attention to Behavior

Coping with the swirling feelings that accompany their parents getting divorced is not easy. Divorce is a loss for children, and they will feel sad and need to grieve. Giving them permission, time, and space to feel sad is necessary. You can do this by being emotionally supportive. You can acknowledge their feelings and let them know it's okay to feel however they feel, because it is. You learned these skills in Chapter 2. Listening without trying to fix or dismiss is amazingly cathartic.

You've heard that children of divorced parents are more likely to have emotional and behavioral difficulties. They seek ways to cope with the changes and feelings. My intention is not to frighten you, but like everything else, to inform you. At the same time, I want you to know that your child doesn't need to be one who fares poorly after a divorce, turning to drugs or alcohol, early sexual activity, or juvenile delinquency. Already you've amassed significant authoritative parenting skills to be the parent your child needs.

Common problems to watch for include academic and behavioral changes at school, mental health changes, and socioeconomic effects.

Be mindful of lower grades and infractions of school rules. Also, at school, they may make new friends whose families look more like their view of themselves. Their connection with extracurricular activities may differ as well. Letting your child's counselor, coaches, and teachers know of the changes in their family dynamics may be helpful.

Because tweens are normally moody and retreat to be by themselves, it's necessary to be extra diligent watching for signs of mental health issues. Your child's mental health needs to be a top priority as usual. Common problems include anxiety, depression, and insomnia. Don't be afraid if you see the signs of these; respond by talking with them and seeking support for them. If you are not sure, ask a professional for advice. The sooner mental health issues are dealt with, the better. Also, please don't take your child's struggle as a sign that you are failing them. When they get a virus, you don't blame yourself, and the same needs to be applied here.

The socioeconomic changes affect children too. When our social circles and/or economics change, we need to accept them with honesty. When you and your ex can no longer afford to send them to the summer camp they love or even pay for them to eat out with their friends like they used to, it's disappointing for them and you. Both parents need to speak gently about these matters.

Sources of Support

Parents going through a breakup often recognize that their child needs more support than they alone can give during this time. Fortunately, there are places where you can find help.

Many schools offer support groups for children of divorced parents. A group atmosphere is good for tweens because peer support matters so much at this age. Remember, your child wants to fit in and feel understood. They don't always want to talk to just another adult but rather to other tweens who can truly understand what they are going through. School counselors are trained in how to facilitate groups so that every child who wants to speak is heard, and those who only want to listen can.

There are also many therapists and coaches who work with adolescents. There is a difference between the two, and your choice will depend upon your child's needs. Therapists can help with healing and overcoming challenges. Coaches can help with building skills and strategies for the future.

What additional support you choose will depend on your child's specific needs. Without experience or tools to cope with a huge shift in their lives, every tween can benefit from extra help during this experience. Trusted adult friends or family members can be wonderfully helpful. It is not a sign that you have failed as a parent—in fact, it is a sign of good parenting to know when to call on additional resources.

Presence

Perhaps above all, your tween needs you to be present and available in their lives. They need to know that you and your love for them are still the same, even though their family looks and feels different. The lifetime familiar nuclear family setup where one parent is cooking in the kitchen, and another is getting out boots for tomorrow's snowstorm has ended. Also missing is the sense of unity that comes from being physically together. So, both parents must create a new sense of normal family and unity in their separate living abodes with the same love.

Even when we cannot be physically present, we can be present in other ways, so our tweens feel connected and see our commitment. You can set aside specific times to touch base each day, such as a goodnight text, a feelings check, having conversations, and showing up for events even when it is not your turn to have them. If you are intentional about being present for your child, they will notice. Such awareness can help them feel that even when so much is in flux, your relationship is constant.

Co-Parenting versus Parallel Parenting

In co-parenting, both parents share similar goals for their children. Their hopes, dreams, values, and vision for their child are grounded and solid. Their strategies for achieving those goals may vary, but they agree on the big picture about launching their children into adulthood with specific talents, education, and beliefs. Most of all, they support each other with respect. Their core values are, for the most part, in sync.

In parallel parenting, there is far less communication and agreement. It's extremely confusing and frustrating for children. Parents act disrespectfully to each other, disagree on many things, and don't share goals. It does not mean either parent loves the child less, but the discord is harmful.

Colin, an eighth grader, is on the Speech and Debate team, but his divorced parents, Matt and Jamie, disagree on his involvement. Matt encouraged this pursuit; he did speech and debate in middle school, making many friends and learning valuable skills. Jamie, however, sees no value in speech and debate and has Colin helping at the family business to learn how it works. Because of this difference, Matt pays for all the competition fees and trips related to it.

One Saturday, Colin is helping Jamie at the family's store. He usually enjoys the work, but this time it means he is missing out on valuable prep time for next week's big debate. Colin tries to review his notes while he is doing some data entry, but Jamie walks in on it.

"What are you looking at?"

"Oh, nothing." Colin slides the notes under the keyboard and tries to shift the subject. "I've almost got this done!"

"That wasn't nothing. Show me." She holds out her hand.

"Is this for debate?" She hands the notes back.

Colin nods. His voice wobbles a little. "I was just taking a quick look. I forgot one of the terms I was trying to memorize. I was still doing my job."

Jamie frowns. "It's fine for you to look at your notes. Why are you acting like I caught you stealing or something?"

"I know how much you hate debate," Colin shrugs. "I know I'm supposed to forget all about it when I'm with you."

"Did your dad say that?"

"No. I figured it out on my own. You and Dad always argue about what I do. I never talk about the store when I'm with Dad because it makes him mad that I work. I try not to talk about debate when I'm with you because you don't think it's important. But the competition next week is important, and it cost Dad a lot of money to send me, so I was trying to look at my notes but not make you mad, only that didn't work, and—" He starts to tear up and stops talking.

Jamie pulls up a chair next to Colin. "I want you to understand."

He knows what she's going to say. But he doesn't care. He's

exhausted from his parents trying to win him over to their side. "Mom, I don't want to talk about it. It's always the same thing. Let me get back to work."

"But it really is okay with me."

"I don't want to talk about it. Leave me alone. I'll get this done."

We can't blame Colin for being exasperated. He knows exactly what his parents think. It feels impossible to please both parents, or even one of them. The lack of cooperation and respect they show each other is toxic to children.

Other examples of harmful parenting include not sharing information, supporting unhealthy eating or exercising habits, not being prompt for exchange time, and not making school, studying, and attendance a priority.

When a parent doesn't consider what is best for their children and fails to cooperate with the other parent, the ongoing opposition causes children to feel uncertain, frustrated, and insecure. It doesn't mean either of them loves their child less, but it does mean that the one-sided parents value their desire to be right and have their way over their child's emotional well-being.

It's important to note, however, that sometimes parallel parenting may be necessary. Abuse, incarceration, and some mental health and substance issues often make parallel parenting a safer and more positive option—and that's okay. You should never feel pressured to co-parent if doing so feels unsafe or damaging for you or your child.

If you've gotten off track on your parenting journey, you are not doomed to continue. You can reach out to your ex and suggest changing. Taking the high road can be life-changing.

Parenting Models to Avoid

Co-parenting has some common pitfalls. The following parenting patterns are easy to fall into but should be avoided.

Disneyland Parent: buys things to win over or gain favor with the child, suggesting that money is more important than love, trust, or respect.

Distant Parent: physically available but does not get emotionally involved; puts up barriers that prevent connecting with their child or maintaining a relationship; may be caused by addiction or by prioritizing a second family over the first one, or work issues.

Driveway Parent: spends as little time as possible with a child so that seeing their child comes across as a duty rather than a pleasure.

Inclusive and Intentional Communication

The communication skills we've discussed throughout this book may be put to the test when you are parenting after a divorce, but effective communication—communication that is open, honest, and empathetic—will always benefit your child. Good communication with your tween *and* with your child's other parent is essential as you embark upon or redefine your family's life.

Keep the Lines Open

When one parent knows something about their child, the other parent should know it too. You don't want to weaponize silence or shut out the other parent, either on purpose or by accident.

For example, if you receive an email from a teacher and see your ex was not included in the list of recipients, forward that message to them. If your child is sick or getting an award or got in trouble at school, tell your ex. Wanting your child to be supported by the other parent is your intention.

Giving your ex the opportunity to know what is going on and to be an equally involved parent benefits your tween. For example, if your child is not passing a class because they have missing work and they will be with your ex for the long weekend, it benefits your child to let your ex know the situation if they don't already so they can make sure the homework gets done.

Share What You See

Communication is not just about passing on schedule details and updates regarding school. It is also about providing your child's other parent with the kinds of observations you would normally share if you were still together.

For example, if you attend your daughter's volleyball practice, it may be obvious to you that you should tell your ex that the time for the upcoming game has changed. But you can also say what you see. You might send a text saying, "Caitlin's serve is so much better today! She increased her percentage, and after one shot, she jumped up and down because she was so happy with what she did!" If you have a video, send it. This is not the time to be selfish or hold things back.

You can also communicate about problems you notice, such as unusual silence ("Is something going on? He's hardly talking to me this evening.") or difficult behavior ("Heads up: they've been snapping at me all day. I think they were up all night at that sleepover.")

Even things that might not seem like a big deal help the other parent stay involved and connected, which is good for your tween. Did they spend the whole break bingeing *Stranger Things* or reading up on the Formula One season? Are they excited about the essay they're writing? Do they have a running joke with their best friend about marshmallows?

The goal is to let the other parent know everything they would know if they still lived with your tween full-time. Do what you can to strengthen their connection. Doing so will encourage the other parent to do the same for you—and then you all benefit.

Ask for What You Need

Asking or being asked by an ex-partner for something needed or wanted for your child is important even if you feel uneasy. Remember: your shared goal is to benefit your child. This common ground lets you give and ask with graciousness and generosity.

When you make requests of your ex with your child in mind, you are giving them a reason to say *yes*. For example, you might ask your ex, "Would you be willing to switch around our Christmas/Thanksgiving schedule? I know you are supposed to have Christmas and I'm supposed to have Thanksgiving this year, but my brother just said he and his kids are going to fly in from Singapore for Christmas week. It will be Dylan's first chance to see them in three years. He's been asking me about when he'd get to spend time with them. This would really be a special opportunity for him if it works for you." By focusing on why the switch would benefit the child, you frame the request as child-centered, which will encourage your ex to make their decision child-centered. Plus, you've also respected them.

Another common time to ask for help is when you are overwhelmed by your parenting duties. When one parent feels so exhausted that they are running on fumes, they should feel okay about asking the other to pitch in: "With my new duties at work, I'm not going to be able to do a good job managing soccer this year. Would you be willing to take over as a team parent?"

Another problem that pops up frequently is differences in economic resources. Rather than making money an issue that limits a child's activities or opportunities, the parent who can be generous should. All the time. And offer, don't make your child or ex ask.

When you and your ex fall into contentious times, the last thing you may want to do is engage with them by asking for help. Reach out to help by asking "What can I do to help you?" or more specifically "Can I take carpool duty for you this week?" Doing this on a regular basis will foster cooperation and may ultimately lessen some of the tension between you. If you can build an environment where both co-parents feel comfortable making requests and know that the other will say yes

166

whenever possible, your child will be the winner. You may not ever fully get to that point, but it's a goal worth pursuing.

Comparisons

A common communication challenge is how to gracefully handle your child comparing you to your ex. For example, "We always drive through Wendy's when Mom picks us up" or "We don't have bedtimes at Dad's on the weekends." Although you may be tempted to react negatively by bad-mouthing the other parent or criticizing your child for raising the issue, the best approach is to remain calm and empathetic. You can say, "I'm glad you like that" or "That makes it special for you." These positive responses bypass judgment and negativity. You are validating your child's positive feelings about how the other parent does things. You want your child to enjoy their time with the other parent and value them.

Keep in mind that you may *hear* an implication that you should be doing what the ex is doing, but your child may be simply making an observation. If they are indeed angling to change your rules, your response leaves it up to them to make the request specific. Such a conversation may go like this:

"We don't have bedtimes at Dad's on the weekends."

"How does bedtime work?"

"We stay up as late as we want! Can we not have bedtimes when we're with you on the weekends too?"

"No, we'll still have bedtimes, but you can enjoy not having them when you're with your dad."

Other comparisons may point out something negative. Your tween might say, "You hardly ever yell at us, but Mom loses it all the time." When you hear something like this, you might be raging inside because you know how much your child hates to be yelled at, but, again, your best bet is to respond with empathy and without judgment. You can say, "I wish it weren't that way" or "That sounds like it's hard to hear." You could also ask an open-ended question, like "How does that make you feel?" Remember that talking about feelings does not make them worse.

And you are not listening to condemn the other parent or make your child feel better. What does happen is that your child feels understood.

In some cases, after a comparison, you may want to follow up by broaching a conversation with your ex to make sure you are continuing to co-parent effectively. Never accusingly, however, and that communication is for the two of you, not for you and your child.

Communicating during Time Apart

Breakups can lead to more time away from your child than you are used to, but intentional communication can help you stay connected. For instance, if you are going on a long business trip, you can ask your child to FaceTime during times you would normally be together. You can tell them, "I'm going to miss you. I want to show you where I am and hear how you are. If you take videos of yourself, please send them and pictures. I'll share where I am with you, too."

You may not be able to attend all their events as you would like if you are traveling. In that case, you might tell them, "I really wish I could be there. I'd love to see a video if anyone takes one." There are many ways to communicate to your child that your heart is with them, even when your physical presence is not possible.

At Your Home

If you are the noncustodial parent, creating a true second home for your child is important. You may be tempted to do this by reestablishing your authority—by being bossy and overdirective—but this strategy is not necessary. And it's not wanted. Your child already knows you are in charge. Instead, be welcoming and show you want them there. Acknowledge that things are different than they used to be and that your home is different from the other parent's.

You could say, "I'm glad you're here! I know it may take a little while for us to get used to things. We're in this together, and I want to know what you would like. Your other parent and I do things differently, but our love is the same." Articulating those ideas and feelings makes it so much easier for your tween to relax and *be* with you.

There are also some basic things you can do to make your home welcoming to your tween. Such little things help them think, *Hey, I'm home here, too!*

Food: Have the food that your tween likes in your home. If they like Cheerios, buy Cheerios, not Rice Chex. If they like cheese sticks, buy cheese sticks. Supply snacks that they can grab and eat without permission, just like at their other home. You want them to be able to open the freezer and find their favorite Popsicles or look on the counter and see their favorite fruit.

Dinner: Prepare food that your child likes and eat dinner together, with the TV off and with phones silenced. Make dinner a time when you are fully present for each other.

Provide their own space: If your tween has their own bedroom in your home, have them help you furnish and decorate it the way they like. Let them choose the comforter, the mirror, and the decorations. This is their sanctuary at your house.

If they don't have a separate bedroom, designate certain spots in your home as theirs, so they don't feel like they are invading your space or need to ask for permission to use certain things. They can dump their backpack here, watch a video here, and do homework over there.

Another small way to make the space feel like it is truly your tween's is to display a photo of them with their other parent someplace, even if you need to put it face down when you are home alone!

Essentials: You won't want your child to have to drag a bag to your home every time they visit. The goal is for your child to feel like they live there, that they are not a guest—this is their home.

Provide a duplicate set of essentials. Store a toothbrush, toothpaste, and other toiletries in your bathroom so they don't need to bring those things when they stay with you. They could also have their own bathroom drawer and towels.

Beyond basic toiletries, keep on hand what your child uses regularly out of necessity or for fun, such as device chargers, sports equipment, and art supplies. Keep some of their clothes there too, as well as cold- and wet-weather gear.

Rules: Your child needs to know your expectations. Your rules don't have to be the same as the other parent's—children are very adept at adapting to different rules in different locations and won't struggle with this—but your tween does need clarity about them. Are they expected to make their bed? Go to sleep at a certain time? What chores are they expected to do? Contributing to the household by doing chores is a wonderful way to help them feel like they belong as they contribute to your household.

Host friends: Help your tween maintain their all-important peer relationships by hosting their friends. If you were the kind of family that had your child's friends sleep over before the divorce, continue that practice. Do whatever you can so your child feels like they belong in your home and has ownership over that environment.

Be ready to deliver items: In Chapter 4, we talked about your child's tween years being the time to end the parent delivery service. But when a child has more than one home, you will need to adjust that practice. They may need that trumpet or iPad before they see you next week. You don't want to separate them from success because they are learning how to juggle two households, so be gracious about returning and delivering needed items.

Get involved in your tween's interests: When you are together, make a point of doing things together that your child likes to do. You don't want your child to come to your house and be ignored or sit idly by, waiting for something to happen because it's your night or weekend to have them. Your time together should be just that: time *together*.

I once had a client who was an avid outdoorsman. He liked fishing, hunting, and yard work. He had no interest in the arts. His daughter was the opposite: she hated being outdoors and loved live theater, especially musicals. When this father made a point of asking his daughter what she wanted to do when they were together, she said, "I want to go to every musical that comes to town." So that's what they did.

He may not have liked musicals, but he liked her and knew that spending time with her doing what she wanted would give them a lot to talk about. It would be a way to deepen their relationship. And he didn't just go through the motions. Not only did they go to a live musical once a month, but beforehand, they went out to dinner so his daughter could explain the plot and give him some background on the show. Sometimes she previewed some songs for him on YouTube. Then, on the way home, they discussed the show.

He told me that before this experience, he had never really understood the value of doing something with his child that she liked, something that she had a passion about when he didn't share it. He gained tremendous insight about his daughter from those nights, and they made lifetime memories.

I encourage you to do something similar: find something your child likes that you can do together. It may be fishing, playing a video game, cooking, trying a Lego challenge, working your way through every *Star Wars* movie and TV show, running, building furniture, learning new dances, or playing laser tag. The activity doesn't matter as much as the fact that you are engaged together doing something your tween finds fun or is passionate about. If you don't initially find the activity interesting, look through your child's eyes: learn what they see in it, and you will learn so much about them.

A New Romance

After a divorce, parents may wonder if there is someone else for them, or if they will be attracted to anyone else. So, when they finally get on a dating app or start a new relationship, it's exciting. But we need to be careful because often after the breakup, parents cleave to their child for a while. After an intense period of closeness, a new romantic relationship can cause your tween to feel pushed aside or abandoned as you explore a new relationship. This is not a case of FOMO; it's feeling replaced and ignored.

You can avoid this problem by carving out a separate space at first for your new romantic life. Plan dates for times when you don't have your child. There is no reason for your child to meet temporary, casual dating partners. You don't even necessarily need to tell them you have begun dating. It's private information—and you don't need to share it with your ex-partner, either. Be careful of time spent texting or talking to this new person.

However, even though your child does not need to immediately be involved in your dating life, it is important to weigh the value of a romantic relationship against what your child needs and how they will be affected. If that relationship will make your child feel disconnected from you, it may not be worth pursuing. If you are attracted to a person who does not like children, that person will want to do things that don't include your child and can challenge your commitment to your children and your values. You don't need them.

If you enter a relationship that looks like it's getting serious, you may reach the point where it's time to introduce your new person to your child. This situation can be tricky. We can't make our child like a person we are attracted to, and we can't make that person like our child. If you have a live-in boyfriend or girlfriend, the dynamics of the household will change considerably, so you need to weigh all the things that could go right and wrong. A small list of things to consider includes clothing that you wear, who can discipline, what that person should be called, and leaving your child alone with this person.

If you decide to remarry, many conversations need to be had and agreements made about the parenting aspects of your relationship. It's possible to create a playbook with values and habits that will be honored. Your guiding principles must be communicated and implemented. You do not want a stepparent to favor their own children over yours, whether in presents given, discipline, privileges granted, or the amount of time spent together. Children and teens keep score of fairness. Life may not be fair overall, but you want your home to be as equitable as you can make it.

If you and your new spouse have children together, you will want to make sure you do not put *all* your energy into that new baby. The older children will still need everything they needed before, and they will also now need reassurance that they are not less important than the newest member of the family. I've seen this go badly, causing the older child to feel rejected and isolated.

Must-Dos for Divorced Parents

Here is some additional practical advice to foster close connections with your tween, even as the shape of your family life changes in the wake of divorce.

Go to every game, performance, presentation, or competition possible. It doesn't matter if it is your day or weekend with your child or not: you need to show up.

Use everyone's favorite device to communicate your love and interest. Do not text during school or past their bedtime.

Hold your ex-partner with kind regards. Follow the golden rule of treating others as you would like to be treated, if for no other reason than to set a positive example for your child.

Support what is happening in your ex's life, whether it is a new job, a new partner, a sick parent, surgery, etc. Help your child be supportive too, such as by taking them to visit your ex in the hospital.

Give the other parent the benefit of the doubt. If they don't show up for something, call or text to see if they're okay rather than assuming they are being negligent or saying to yourself, "Yay, I get the kids to myself!"

Don't forget about their other grandparents. Your ex's family still loves your children, and it's important to foster those relationships. If they spent a week with them each summer, let that continue. If Aunt Maribel takes them to the fair each year, let her continue.

Be reliable and on time when exchanging children. It will build trust and reliability with your children and your ex. Plus, your children will see that you respect each other and each other's time.

Think ahead about what may be difficult for your tween to understand or adjust to, and talk about these things. The first year of the divorce is all about new routines, particularly around holidays and other family traditions. It can be challenging to navigate. For example, your traditional summer trip to the lake will be different without Dad attending. To prepare your child for this change, you might say, "Your dad's not going to be there to drive the speedboat this summer. Uncle Ben is joining us again this year. He volunteered to drive the boat and help you water-ski. Would that be okay with you?" The reality is that things are different, so it is important to talk about and acknowledge it, so your child doesn't have to deal with unwelcome surprises.

Co-Parenting in Action: Kiana's Story

As hard as we may try, not every interaction with our ex-partner will go smoothly. We are all imperfect people; we all make mistakes. Remember Kim and Darrin from the start of this chapter? Fortunately, they both want to co-parent successfully, so they both work to find common ground after their communication stumbles.

That Tuesday morning, as you may recall, Kim's phone lit up with a text as she drove Kiana to school, and she asked her daughter to read it out for her.

"It's Dad," Kiana reported. "He said, 'Just wanted to see if Kiana will actually be at her piano lesson later. Asking now because I know your day might get too *hectic* to send me any updates.'" Kiana rolled her eyes. "I thought you said you two weren't going to be mean to each other anymore."

Kim sighed. "You're right. I should have talked to him again about last week. I'll call him as soon as I get to work."

And she did. Once he answered, she began by apologizing, making sure it was a true apology. "I'm sorry I didn't tell you last week when Kiana got sick, and I'm sorry I wasn't more understanding when you called that evening. I was inconsiderate of your time and made you worry for no reason. It probably reminded you of other times I kept things from you. I really didn't intend to keep you out of the loop this time, but I did. I promise to do better prioritizing telling you about what is going on with our daughter. Can you forgive me?"

There was a pause. Darrin was not entirely over his anger, but he knew he needed to move forward for Kiana's sake. "I forgive you," he said. "And you're right. I felt really left out. But I also could have been more understanding because I know you get stressed when Kiana is sick.

So, I'm sorry I snapped at you and sent a mocking text this morning. I should have been more considerate and not assumed the worst of you."

"I forgive you too. There are a couple things for tonight, Darrin. Please remind Kiana to take her antibiotics at dinner, because they need to be taken with food. And she's probably going to ask if she can have a milkshake tonight like usual, but even if she takes her Lactaid, the meds are messing up her stomach, so please say *no*."

Darrin laughed. "Definitely."

"Also, she's been really frustrated learning that new Beethoven sonata, and she's nervous the teacher is going to think she didn't practice enough."

"I'll ask her after the lesson how it went. And did she tell you Grace is going to sleep over this weekend?" Darrin had been working hard to make his place feel like home for his daughter.

"Oh good! They haven't spent much time together lately."

"Well, I'm glad we're back on track," Darrin said after another brief pause.

"Me too."

The very best thing Kim and Darrin did is remember and follow what they agreed on: they want to make Kiana's life the best it can be and honor each other as parents.

Key Takeaways

The goal of co-parenting is to make life go smoothly for your tween. To do so, you and your ex need to agree on and live by the shared values and goals for your child. It is helpful to remember that your relationship with your child and your ex is as important as ever with the **Trio of Trials** continuing to shape their growth, and they need you.

By providing the continuity, empathy, and support that your child needs; by doing what you can to make your home welcoming even when it is their secondary residence; by communicating effectively with your child and ex; and by being thoughtful about new romances, you will go a long way toward easing life for your tween being the child of divorced parents. Your shared goals for your child will help you navigate any conflicts.

Your Key Takeaways: Your Turn to Write
Name three things you learned.

1. _____

2. _____

3. _____

Name two awarenesses you'll embrace.

1. _____

2. _____

Name at least one thing you will apply. What will you do differently?

1. _____

And remember, even when we do our best to help our children through difficult situations, they may face a crisis that requires professional help. Understanding your tween's mental health needs is a crucial part of parent leadership in today's world. We'll discuss this in the next chapter.

Chapter 9
Mental Health – Making it a Priority for Your Tween and You

Liam's dad, Dennis, was excited when he came home. "Liam! We're all set! We're going to the game!" He smiled at his wife, Stacey, in the kitchen. "My buddy came through—two seats in the midfield!"

"At last! Something that will pull our son out of his eighth-grade funk!" she grinned.

But when Liam came in, wearing the same shirt as the day before, he said, "That's okay, Dad. You can take someone else. I'm not in the mood."

"But it's for the championship, and you love this team. We both do."

Liam shrugged. "Next time, Dad." He headed off to his room, shutting the door behind him. His parents knew what he was doing: lying on his bed, staring at the wall, and ignoring his phone, books, saxophone—all the things that, until recently, seemed to bring him joy.

"I told him I was making chicken piccata," Stacey said, "and he just shrugged at that, too, like it hasn't been his favorite meal since he was five."

"I still think he had a fight with Mason and Alexis." Dennis chewed his bottom lip. "This must be the longest he's gone without hanging out with them."

"He said he didn't." Stacey turned around and leaned her back against the counter. "He said he just hasn't felt like seeing them. And he's tired."

"Even though he's sleeping ten hours a night." Dennis shook his head. "I'm worried."

"My mom says it's growing pains." Stacey scratched her head. "Maybe we should just give him space. I mean, we're good parents. It's not like anything could be seriously wrong, right?" When Dennis didn't answer, she looked directly at him. "Right?"

"I don't know anymore."

Liam's parents knew him. They could sense he was struggling. Now they had to decide their next step.

Mental Health Matters

It's easy to think of mental health as a secretive and mysterious part of the brain's inner workings. Often, its invisibility complicates it. Yet we can agree that unknowns aren't nearly as frightening once we take the time to understand them. As such, we are charged with learning about and accepting that mental health is a vibrant part of what makes us tick—and being prepared to recognize the warning signs of mental illness so we can be ready to respond.

Mental health includes our emotional, social, and psychological well-being. It informs how we feel, act, and think. It influences our coping mechanisms, relationships with others, and decision-making. It determines our capacity to be our best self at school, home, and with every interaction. It is intertwined with our physical health and is just as important.

Mental illness is a state of non-well-being and refers collectively to mental disorders and conditions exhibited by the inability to think, process emotions, and respond appropriately to all stimuli. Just like physical illnesses, mental illness is nothing to be ashamed of, it is treatable, and it is manageable.

Mental Health: Why It Matters for Tweens

Promoting good mental health is important because it affects our tweens' everyday life, how they respond, and their ability to be resilient. It also determines what they believe to be true about themselves and their world. They act on and emote from that perspective. It's their reality.

Mental health is particularly acute for tweens because, as we know, they are already taxed with the **Trio of Trials**: going through **Puberty**, **Searching for Identity**, and living with their slowly maturing **Immature Prefrontal Cortex**. Having a positive sense of self, confidence, and outlook provides a strong foundation for the tasks required for adulting. We know plenty of learning opportunities pop up along the way, and they need to be mentally healthy to maximize their journey to adulthood.

With all that is going on, tweens question themselves because they feel weird. Often, they don't even know what normal is anymore. They are not the same person they were just six months ago. And it doesn't really make sense to them, and often to us. Understanding how mental health works and how to support theirs will enable you to reassure your tween that feeling "abnormal" is oftentimes perfectly normal.

One of the hardest things for us as parents is being able to differentiate between our tweens' normal challenges and possible mental illness. Is their isolation from not making the team and feeling left out normal? Or is it an unhealthy response? Is the stress from taking more challenging classes okay, or is their response not healthy as they spend less time sleeping and have less fun? There may be a lot of normal in there, but you know your child best, so use your knowledge, insights, and observation as the yardstick. If you suspect your child's mental health is declining, get support. Later in this chapter you'll find a list of mental illness warning signs. You will not regret paying close attention.

If it seems like you have even more responsibilities than before, you do. I want you to feel brave and confident because your response and concern about mental health make a huge difference. If in doubt, ask for help. Knowledge is power. I think I've mentioned this before.

Consider These Signs of Good Mental Health in Tweens:

- Feeling happy
- Feeling positive about themselves
- Enjoying life
- Bouncing back from upsets and disappointments
- Maintaining strong relationships with family and friends
- Participating in physical activity
- Eating a healthy diet
- Possessing a sense of achievement
- Being able to relax and get needed sleep
- Feeling a sense of belonging at school, at home, with friends, and with family
- Voicing positive beliefs about themselves and the world
- Dealing with stress in positive ways

Possessing these qualities empowers your tween to negotiate life's obstacles and enjoy life's pleasures. You can be confident that their self-image and worldview enable them to find successes in everyday life. They are equipped with a mindset to face and resolve conflicts easily. Practice helps, outlook helps, and support helps. It's what your child believes and how they perceive and process what happens that matters.

The following contribute to your child's mental health:

Does your child have at least one good friend? One good friend, a peer who believes in your tween and likes to do the things they like to do, is a must for getting through these challenging years. If your tween does not seem to have a friend they truly trust and who truly trusts them back, they may feel isolated and alone. They are too old for you to arrange playdates, but you can encourage them and remind them how to make a friend and be a friend.

Does your child have at least one adult besides you whom they can talk to? This adult may be another relative or someone else in their community. An adult who knows your tween and who can provide wise support is invaluable. If your tween does not seem to have such an adult, ask your child if there are adults they trust and if they'd value talking with them. You can't force this, but you can look for opportunities with trusted friends and family members.

Does your child have at least one activity that gives them opportunities to gain confidence, find success, or strive for mastery? This would be an activity that gives your tween a chance to think, learn, move, or develop competency. It could be an organized school activity such as band or a sport, or it could be in an area of interest like caring for a pet or hiking. It doesn't matter whether your child is the best at this activity; it matters that they are engaged and enjoy it.

Does your child have a secure home life with at least one parent who shows them love and affection, and provides shelter, food, clothing, and protection? This may seem like it's a given, but still, it needs to be mentioned. Having a parent who spends time with them, hears them, and shows up contributes to their mental health.

Does your child have an autonomy mindset, and are they able to ask for help? If so, they show signs of self-sufficiency and are confident solving their own problems. They monitor their actions and behavior as they interact with peers and adults. And when they have a problem, they are comfortable asking for help.

Throughout this book, we talk about relationship-building with your tween as you develop your leadership approach. You'll recall: not the boss, but a trusted collaborator, as an example. They don't want to be told what to do, but they do want to be heard and acknowledged. They want to be a decision-maker in their own life, even though they do not have access to the same decision-making skills as adults do. Practicing with your tween forges these skills, even the how-to-respond-to-stress skills. No one moment will capture whether they are mentally healthy. But your sustained relationship and insight provide the intel to help you measure.

Consider this scenario with seventh grader Kobe:

Kobe's math class was released early for lunch. Spontaneously, without uttering a word, the race to the cafeteria was on, each student vying to be the first one in the lunch line to secure bragging rights. Kobe is in the lead. As he rounds the last corner at the end of the hall, he trips and falls flat on the floor, in front of all his classmates.

Version 1:

His face hot, Kobe sits up but stays on the floor, looking down until the rest of the class runs past him. Then he walks to the nurse's office, even though he isn't hurt. If he hides in there, he thinks, no one will tease or ridicule him.

Version 2:

Kobe pops to his feet and says with a grin, "The ground came out of nowhere!" The other kids laugh with him. He trots along to lunch, cheering on his friends as they continue to race to be first.

Neither version of Kobe would reveal the full state of his mental health, but as parents, you know which version you hope your child is. Good mental health means tweens are more often able to respond like the second Kobe. To be resilient and recover quickly from unintended occurrences. The other thing is that successfully managing the conflict brings confidence for the next time. It becomes a mindset.

What determines which Kobe a child will be? His mental health and experiences determine it.

When the first Kobe fell, he didn't believe he could stand up or keep going. He let his trip define him—he became the mistake, the kid who fell. He internalized the situation; he didn't feel like he belonged to his tribe at that moment. He felt alone and that he stuck out. It didn't matter that his peers liked him—what mattered was what he believed. He was embarrassed and self-conscious.

When the second Kobe fell, he believed it was no big deal. He defined himself not by the fall but by his reaction to it—his eagerness to make a joke, laugh at himself, and invite others to laugh with him. He believed they would laugh with him and not at him. He saw himself as someone who could make things happen—control who he wanted to be. The fall was what he *went through*, not who he was.

Most tweens could be either of the two Kobes, depending on how any day is going, but a child with stronger mental health will more likely have the belief system that lets them bounce back.

Supporting Your Tween's Mental Health

Self-care is a key component in mental health for adults and children. And, as the saying goes, parents need to put their own masks on first.

Modelling Your Self-Care: Your Mindset Activities

When you hear the term "self-care," you might think of bubble baths or golf outings. Even though these count as self-care, the day-to-day version is neither luxurious nor always fun. Self-care is not selfish, but it is necessary to support and boost our own mental health.

I encourage you to add these practices to your life. When we believe we don't have time, or put everyone else's needs in front of ours, or when we try to always keep all the balls in the air, something we don't want to happen could easily happen. By practicing the self-care tips below, you maintain and support your emotional and mental health. Your children see this and learn from you.

I urge you to add these practices to your self-care.

Honoring yourself. This includes maintaining boundaries and being compassionate with yourself. When you recognize your strengths and weaknesses, set and keep boundaries, and speak kindly to yourself, you nurture the best version of yourself. You can then be kindly and gently honest with yourself about mistakes and successes. You can embrace that you, like everyone else, are an imperfect person. You get to be you with both your wins and warts. With no shame, you are YOU.

Move, move, move. Regular exercise boosts your mood, increases concentration, and improves physical and mental health. Increasing your heart rate, stretching your muscles, and freeing up your mind give you energy. You don't need to run a marathon—try a fifteen-minute walk, a YouTube yoga workout, swimming, or climbing up and down the stairs in your office building. Make moving a priority because it is.

Eat healthy. It can be hard to make good food choices all the time. When you make incremental improvements, you'll create a better relationship with food, and over time you will feel the benefits. A friend shared that she doesn't buy those items she can't stay away from—then she can't eat or drink them. An additional benefit is that we get a dopamine ping when we recognize each positive choice. Walking past the ice cream aisle without throwing a carton in the cart is an example of giving yourself credit—thus the ping!

Sleep. It's a superpower. Part of good sleep practice is turning off all devices with screens an hour before bed, going to bed about the same time every night, keeping your bedroom dark, and maintaining a cool temperature. Create a bedtime routine where you slow down before you go to bed rather than running around doing a hundred things before sliding under the covers with your brain still analyzing the list of what you forgot and what needs attention first thing in the morning. Rather, ease yourself into resting time with a shower or bath, pamper your face and skin, put on nightwear that is comfortable, and then get in your made bed relaxed and ready to sleep.

Connect with others. We are social beings who need human connections. We need to be seen, heard, and understood—and to see, hear, and understand others. Relationships expand when we are there for the other person, have fun together, and work toward the same goals. Positive friendship and family connections fulfill our lives and meet our needs for socialization.

Ask for help when you need it. Connections with others are also important because we know we can rely on each other and not feel like we must do it all alone. People like to help. If you say to a friend, "I know I said I'd bring dessert to the party, but I can't get there. Can you stop and pick up a cherry pie?" the likely response will be, "No worries, I've got your back." Let yourself ask for and receive help. This includes professional help for physical or mental health support.

Practice relaxing. When you have spent a day with clients or team members whose problems seem insurmountable, or with a boss whose demands match her bad temper, or at home with your uncooperative tween, you may be tempted to keep working on solutions after the workday ends. Don't do it. Instead, let it all go—you need to disconnect. It is mentally healthy to emotionally separate and physically step away from the stresses so you can unwind. For some people, that means walking after work, listening to or playing music, vegging out in front of the TV, or engaging in a hobby. Knowing and doing those things that empower you to let go of stress have the added benefit of feeding your spirit and soul, soothing your restlessness, and restoring your mojo and peace.

Pause and breathe. Think about the power of the pause button on your TV remote when you have to pee, get a snack, or drive your tween to scouts. You have your own pause button in your brain. Temporarily stop what is going on and redirect yourself to something that replenishes you. You know how good it feels when you take deep breaths and feel the oxygen energize you. Or walk away from a project when you're stuck and the ideas won't come. Powering down with a pause is just as useful as powering up.

When a Parent Is Struggling with Their Mental Health

Maybe depression, anxiety, or mood swings challenge you. Maybe recent layoffs at work have triggered anxiety or you are still not engaged socially as much as you were before COVID. Maybe you recognize you are drinking more than before. Maybe you fly off the handle in response to small and large stressors. When you take the time to examine your life and ask those you trust to weigh in, changes can be observed and recognized. In each of these examples, it's necessary to check in with a mental health professional. In reaching out for support, please realize it is a strength, because it is. Accepting the problem as real and acting on it will be helpful. Hoping you'll feel better doing nothing promises nothing.

As the number one person in your child's life—the true perspective, not necessarily theirs—your mental health needs must be attended to all the time.

Your mental health grows by doing the following:

- Practicing self-care.
- Reaching out to a mental health professional (for a new condition) or checking in regularly with your provider (for an ongoing condition).
- Being patient with yourself as you address your issues, especially if medication is involved: it can take time to find the right medication.
- Asking for help and saying no when you need to.
- Stay connected with your tribe and support system

Ways to Help Your Tweens

Supporting your tween's mental health may seem like a daunting task, but every chapter in this book is in fact about just that. Just as you teach your children to study, brush their teeth, and use good phone etiquette, you must teach them how to care for their mental health as well. Your relationship with them and your new leadership skills contribute to this. You communicate well by listening, being empathic and curious. You collaborate to make shared decisions. You talk openly about all things related to sexuality. You give and receive second chances. You regulate your emotions. You teach your child how to balance responsibilities and privileges.

In addition, please consider that another foundation of mental health lies in meeting your tween's basic needs for food, water, warmth, rest, physical safety, and personal relationships. These are at the base of Maslow's hierarchy of needs. It is much easier to be mentally healthy growing up, and to be who you are supposed to be, when the basics are assured.

The suggestions below create a healthy and nurturing environment.

Set a positive tone. You can adopt an attitude that suggests the future is hopeful and approachable. Even though problems exist, you and your tween can deal with them. Help them realize that their choice of actions makes a difference. What is going on in the world cannot be ignored, but you choose how you respond to it and its availability in your home. For instance, instead of binge-watching a TV show or having the news on 24-7, create a peaceful place to share the day and relax. Realizing that they can make choices that affect their own lives is very powerful for children.

Create joy. Sometimes we forget about just having fun. Joy feeds our spirit and mental health, just like moving our bodies does. Show your child love in the way they like to receive it. Stop to greet them with a smile and some time when they come home. Share a snack and have a chat without asking yes-and-no questions. Play a new video game, listen to each other's favorite songs, walk the dog together, or share photos or videos from your phone. Look for joy in places big and small. Smile and laugh more.

Ensure that there are support systems in place for your tween. Your presence and attentiveness demonstrate that you care and will be there for them no matter what. You can talk about ways to cope, such as calling a friend, listening to music, writing, or making art. And it's important that they have a person of their choosing whom they can call at any time to support them in any way without judgment. Decide on a secret code word to say or text when they need help. No questions asked.

Accept your child for who they are. Your tween may not be who you expected or wanted them to be. They may not live out all the dreams you had for them (or be able to live out your unfulfilled dreams). But they are still their wonderful, unique selves. Accepting does not mean you do not guide, encourage, and support them, but it does mean you understand that your artistically minded tween may not be the doctor you always dreamed of having in the family, or that your child who does Tae Kwan Do is not going to lead the basketball team to a championship the way you did. If they feel your acceptance, they will better be able to accept themselves and do well.

A mom I was coaching was confused when her daughter wanted to go thrifting. They could afford whatever she needed. This mom acquiesced with grace. On their way to the store, her daughter told her about sweatshops, the overproduction of goods, and other problems with "fast fashion." If she bought clothes at the thrift store, she would not be contributing to the problem and could give the money she saved to food banks. "Why should you overpay for clothes when I can get something that looks good, has hardly been worn, and costs next to nothing?" By saying *yes* when she wanted to override and dismiss thrifting, this mom affirmed her daughter, her values, and her beliefs.

The Power of Emotions

Emotions provide us with insight and information as well as a physical presence. In the old days, when we saw a tiger, the immediate danger triggered an instant release of adrenaline and cortisol. The message was to run for safety. Fast. Today the same thing happens when we are faced with danger. Only the danger is not the tiger; it's the grade or a breakup or test anxiety or millions of other frightening things that we become uniquely attuned to in a flash.

The visceral response to emotions is not limited to the scary stuff. Our hearts beat wildly when we are attracted to someone or when we want to supply the answer in class. Or when we think about how fun something will be, and we anticipate the excitement of it.

As introduced in Chapter 1, here's how it works. Something happens and the limbic system is notified. An emotion or more than one is then attached to the event. The emotion(s) tied to the event ends up either being a bottleneck or a sieve. The event can either stay stuck in the limbic system or go on to the cognitive processing center where the person then deals with the event and is not limited by or tied to the emotion.

The emotions attached to an event can be confusing. They can be subjective and one-sided. Just as they were for the version of Kobe who couldn't deal with the embarrassment of tripping. For all of us, the emotional perception can be nebulous. Yet these bits of emotional information shape our experiences, our relationships, our sense of self, and our responses. They can make or break, limit or enhance, empower or motivate, and encourage or hobble action all together. But the thing is we can learn from emotions and our responses to them.

We do not need to idly stand by, imprisoned by emotions attached to events. The second Kobe had a mindset where he was comfortable in his own skin—and his tripping was not going to define him as a negative thing—he took charge of the event and his emotional response to it. We each get to decide how to respond to every event just as Kobe did. One choice was limited by his emotions, and the other took positive action by moving from the emotions to cognitively processing how he'd respond. And then he did.

Knowing how to respond and not get bogged down by emotions is a strength evident in good mental health. The more this happens, the more habitual positive responses become. Unfortunately, the reverse is true as well.

As an example, a student hopes that she will get to report on the *fashion and hairstyles of women and men during the Revolutionary War*. These kinds of assignments make history palatable for her. When another student picks it first, her limbic system attaches emotions to it. She feels frustrated that she didn't get the fashion assignment and tells herself the picking process is unfair. Adrenaline, a hormone, kicks in to fan the fury, justify her intensity, and name her emotions. It's a powerful experience that happens to all of us all the time. Adrenaline actuates every emotion.

But then, only then, this student catches herself and recognizes her internal emotional rumination: the negative self-talk. Her cognitive function knows the picking process was arbitrary, and that her internal ranting is not changing anything. She recognizes that being powerless over this one thing is not the end of everything. This helps her to move on and self-soothe so she can look at the choices remaining and be ready when it is her turn.

Breaking this down: something happened, there was an emotion, there was a hormonal response, and there was a cognitive response.

When we don't connect to that cognitive response—when we stay stuck in our intense adrenaline and the limbic system's response—we end up over agonizing and reliving the event packed with intensity. All too often, this negative self-talk pattern can lead to long-term inability to deal effectively with emotions, let alone events.

> **What we don't want is for our child to develop a negative and pervasive belief that things will go badly, or let unhealthy thinking and emotional processing overpower reasoning.**

What we want to do in helping our children move over to the cognitive is to never doubt their reality, perception, or emotions. Acknowledge these things as real and as their experience. Let them tell the story of the event and how they felt. Accept that how they felt is essential. It is not necessary for us to feel like they feel—in fact, keep your feelings out of it altogether. Curiously, ask for clarification and information. Ask if they are still angry and how they'd like your help. If they are ready to let it go, help them. The goal is to learn resilience and avoid falling into an unhealthy emotional rabbit hole.

This generation has seen *Frozen* a million times, and that pivotal scene where Elsa sings "Let It Go." That serves as a lifetime metaphor when we know how to do it.

Getting Help for Mental Illness

Despite everything parents do to promote mental health, our children may still face mental illness due to chemical imbalances, environmental factors you cannot control, or other unseen or unpredictable factors.

Mental illness is no one's fault. You should not blame yourself or anyone else. Sometimes tweens are affected by events over which we have no control, like the COVID pandemic, or by unavoidable life changes such as moving to a new town. It is important to understand that mental illness in no way indicates any failure on your part, and that anything you have done to support your tween's mental health has put them in the best possible position to cope with what they are now facing.

Facing the possibility that your child is mentally ill can be frightening. It's normal to have strong feelings when a child talks about feeling worthless and wanting to commit suicide, or refuses to go to school, or tells you they hate you or that they hear voices. Sometimes parents are immobilized because the idea of their child suffering is too much to bear. Denial and making your pain the point is the worst possible approach.

You love your child enough to get help. You recognize that dealing with the problem means your child does not need to continue to suffer. Once you know or suspect a problem exists, you work to find support. Not just for your child but for you, too, so you can help them.

Many celebrities have shared their struggles with anxiety, depression, panic attacks, addiction, and more. Many of us had mistakenly assumed the lives of superstars were ideal and perfect, but many have candidly revealed that this is not the case. Their intention is to inspire and persuade their fans who struggle with the same mental illnesses to get help, to realize the problem is treatable, and to take a page from their playbook. They are proof positive that you can go on and do anything despite what you might be going through at any given moment.

Warning Signs

Know the warning signs for mental illness. They include but are not limited to the following:

- Increased isolation, less socializing, change in friends
- Loss of interest in things they used to do or enjoy
- Unexplained aches or pains that don't go away
- Changes in academic performance or engagement
- Inability to concentrate or complete tasks that once were easy
- Thoughts or talk of suicide
- Irrational beliefs and fears—someone or something is trying

to control them
- Restlessness, sleeping too much or too little, or low energy
- Participating in destructive or risky behavior like drinking, smoking, drugs, or promiscuity
- Dieting or exercising excessively and concerns about weight gain

If or when you become aware of your child exhibiting these, be watchful and take the needed action. You recognize changes because you know your children. You can also rely on the observations from other adults in your family as well as coaches, teachers, and friends' parents. You can readily tell the difference between your child's typical bad moods of **Puberty** and the above warning signs.

A student of mine, Braden, usually makes straight As, but this quarter every grade is a C- or lower. When he comes to my office we chat and then I say, "Help me understand what's going on. I'm seeing something different this grading period. You've always loved learning and are willing to work hard. Something is different now."

At first, he shakes his head, denying anything is going on, but then I ask him how his parents have reacted to the change. He rolls his eyes. "All they do is take away my phone privileges and ground me from seeing my friends."

"That's hard for you, right?"

"All they care about is my good grades." He gives me the man nod, but I hear a hitch in his voice.

"And you think that's *all* they care about?" I ask gently.

That question breaks the dam. Braden explains to me how it seems like his parents just want someone to brag about. He says they go on and on to their friends and relatives about his latest test scores and achievements. They never talk about him being a good leader, being organized, or being helpful in the church nursery. "It's like I'm a robot. They expect me to perform and perform, and they never see how hard I'm working or ask me if it is important to me to be a good student. So, I decided I'd stop being one and see if they noticed me, not my grades. To see if they'd still love me if I was a failure."

"And how's the experiment going?"

He shakes his head and looks at the ceiling.

"Do you want to tell your parents how you feel?"

"I don't think they want to know,"

"But you'd like them to know, right?" I ask.

He nods.

The next day, his parents come in and the four of us talk. They are surprised and concerned about how Braden has been feeling. They had no idea this was his perception. They assure him they love *him*, not his achievements. They apologize for not recognizing him and all that he didn't do to get their attention. The three of them go on to have a much better understanding of each other.

This story serves as a wake-up call for us to realize that our perception of our children and what we project to them or about them can backfire. Braden's story is an example of how an early warning sign can prevent problems from getting worse: if he continued down the path of not communicating with his parents, ignoring his schoolwork, and even disconnecting from his friends as his privileges were taken away, his mental health could deteriorate.

When you talk to your tween about what you see and your concerns, it's important to not label it as a "hard conversation." Even if the subject may be difficult, your words need to be gentle, kind, affirming, understanding, and curious. We never want to assume that they have "something wrong with them." Rather, be concerned about them as a person, as your child. An open approach works best, as well as accepting what they share.

The open-ended questions we discussed in Chapter 2 will be exceptionally helpful here. Instead of asking them to defend and explain themselves, you are asking for information and for their point of view. You might say: "What are you feeling about this...?" or "Have you been thinking about...?" Your approach and language affect the response you receive.

It's more than okay to acknowledge that your child is having a tough time. Don't bother promising things will get better, even though you want to. You can't keep that kind of promise. And it's dangerously close to glossing over or pretending their big issue isn't a big deal. Breathe and listen without judging, and don't insert your fears, even when what they say makes you uncomfortable. Your child trusts you with their feelings and experience.

Primary care doctors are a logical place to begin seeking mental health support for nonemergencies. After a consultation, they may recommend therapy, taking medication, or seeing a psychiatrist. In an emergency, such as threatening suicide, go straight to an ER that has a mental health department. You may need to practice patience during this process: mental health issues often require time to diagnose and treat successfully. It's neither quick nor easy. But it is necessary.

If your tween has a mental illness diagnosis, keep in mind that the future is still wide open. In most cases, it is not a life sentence. Some illnesses are short term, some illnesses improve as a young person matures, and some may need to be treated longer. Mental illness is not a stop of growth for your child; it's a bump on the way to becoming the remarkable person they are meant to be.

I understand that this is not easy. But your child's mental health is essential. I believe in your ability to lead them through this interruption.

Application of Mental Health: Liam's Story

In Liam's story, his parents' observations alerted them that something was not right. They were tempted to let things go and assume it was just part of adolescence.

Dennis put his arm around his wife's shoulder. "As much as I hate to say it, I think we need to have a conversation with Liam and see what's going on."

Stacey leaned her head into him. "I think you're right."

They planned and then waited until after dinner when Liam's younger siblings were in bed. They sat together at the kitchen table.

"Am I in trouble?" Liam asked nervously.

"Absolutely not," Dennis said. "But we wanted to check in with you because we're worried. We've noticed you haven't been doing some of the things you used to enjoy, like playing your sax and watching soccer with me on TV."

Liam shrugged. "I don't feel like it."

"And that's fine." Stacey leaned over the table to take his hand. "We know you're at an age when your interests might change. But we wondered if you've been worried about anything, or thinking hard about something that you might want to share with us."

Liam shrugged again and looked at the table. "Not really."

"Okay," Dennis tried. "We've also noticed you've been extra tired lately. And that you haven't spent much time with Mason and Alexis. You three have always been tight."

Liam frowned. "I don't want to spend time with them."

"Can you help me understand this?" Stacey eyebrows raised higher on her forehead.

Then, it came out. Liam described how at lunch, his two friends had started referring to things he didn't know about, jokes he hadn't heard, plans he'd been left out of. He caught them looking at each other in weird ways. "And then I found out they had their own text chat—without me! Only because it happened to flash on Mason's phone when he asked me to hold it while he was picking up his fork."

It turned out that Mason and Alexis had become a romantic couple and only told Liam after he saw that text message. He had been feeling left out, hurt, and lonely for a month.

"You couldn't have seen that coming. No wonder you've been feeling so bad." Dennis touched him on the shoulder.

"Everything's a mess," Liam said. "I'm so mad at myself for feeling like this!"

"We're concerned about you, Liam." Stacey explained how they could talk to his pediatrician, who could provide some assistance with his mood.

"Wait a second!" Liam opened his eyes wide. "You think I'm *crazy*?"

"Not at all, son." Dennis stood behind him, placed his hands gently on his shoulders. "I think you're going through a rough patch, and it might help to talk to someone who's an expert in rough patches."

"What do you know about this?"

"Remember, I shared with you that when my mom died when I was in college, I saw a therapist for a while. It would be like that. It helped me to talk to someone who knows how feelings and thoughts work. He really helped. I got back to feeling like myself."

"But what if my therapist says I'll just feel like this forever?"

Stacy shook her head. "Then they wouldn't be a very good therapist. We can find one you like. It's worth a try—right?"

"Yeah, that's a good point, I guess." An almost smile appeared on Liam's face. "I'll go."

Dennis and Stacey were on the right track getting help for Liam. If he didn't like the first therapist, they would find another one.

Key Takeaways

We can establish a solid foundation for good mental health by accepting our children for who they are, supporting them, and helping them be their best selves.

Mental health is just like physical health in that it affects our tweens' lives. The **Trio of Trials** can make mental health particularly complicated for tweens and us, but there are still many ways we can promote their mental health through our approach and leadership.

Be mindful of changes in your child, know the warning signs of mental illness, and approach your child kindly and respectfully when expressing your concerns and getting support in place.

Your Key Takeaways: Your Turn to Write

Name three things you learned.

1. _____

2. _____

3. _____

Name two awarenesses you'll embrace.

Loving the Alien

1. _____

2. _____

Name at least one thing you will apply. What will you do differently?

1. _____

Chapter 10
The Daily Routines—Connecting Points in Ordinary Events

Shopping in the store for the week's groceries on Sunday afternoon, Eli's mom, Rachel, looked at the app where family members list what they need. She saw that Eli asked for seven packages of Oreos. *Ha!* she thought. *Nice try, Eli, but you are getting the usual: one.*

Eli was at a friend's house when she got home, so she put the cookies in the pantry and forgot all about them. She barely even saw Eli that evening because he ate dinner at his friend's house, and then he fell asleep while she put his little sister, Willa, to bed.

The next morning as Rachel dressed Willa for preschool, she heard Eli wail, "Noooooooooo!"

Downstairs, she found him standing in the pantry.

"Where are the Oreos?" he asked, a frantic look on his face.

She pulled the package off the shelf. "Please don't scare me like that! I thought something was terribly wrong. They're right here."

"I saw that one, but where are the *others*?" he snapped.

"Please stop yelling at me. What others?"

"I put seven packages of Oreos on the list, and you only bought one!" He freaked out. "I promised I'd bring them. Everyone's going to make fun of me, and I'm going to fail the lab!"

By this point, Eli's dad, Roger, with Willa in hand, had come into the kitchen, drawn by the commotion.

"Son," Roger commanded Eli's attention. "I don't know what the problem is, but I don't like how you're talking to your mother."

Eli gritted his teeth and lowered his voice. "I put seven packages of Oreos on the grocery list because I signed up to bring them for the lab today—"

"What lab?" Roger interrupted.

"My science lab," Eli almost growled. "But Mom only bought one. I have science first period. And I'm going to be in trouble."

"Oh!" Rachel realized what had happened. "I am so sorry, Eli, but I thought you were joking when you put down seven. You did not tell me—"

"I didn't know I was supposed to! When I ask you to buy something you always say, 'Don't *tell* me. Put it on the *list*.'" He mimicked his mom.

Roger glowered. "Stop being rude. It was a simple mistake."

"But *she* doesn't have to go in and tell everyone we can't do a lab because I don't have the Oreos!" Eli shouted.

"Do not refer to me as *she*," Rachel shouted back, shaking her finger.

"You don't even care that you've ruined my whole week!" Eli grabbed his backpack and stormed out of the kitchen.

"Come back here!" Roger yelled.

"No. I'm not going to be late catching the bus."

With the crack of the door slamming, Willa burst into tears.

Eli and his family were off to a particularly rough start to their week—all because of a breakdown in communication.

Creating Reliable Connections

Parents cannot possibly anticipate every situation with their tweens, yet you can establish a paradigm for applying all that you've gained from this book to your family. By building intentional routines and habits into each day, you create rules, expectations, and a sense of belonging that increase trust and communication. All your common and ordinary occasions are yours to seize.

When we heard Dorothy say, "There's no place like home," we knew exactly what she meant. Parents provide so much more than the basics of food, shelter, and clothing. No matter what happens at work, school, or the piano recital, family members return to the comfort of this safe place. Here they are replenished, loved, accepted, seen, and heard. Home with their family is the place where your tween gets to be themself—sometimes their best and other times their worst—with you.

Your children learn your values, beliefs, and rules not by accident but because you live them every day. In your family, everyone knows where they stand, that they are accepted, and how they fit. Let's talk about this template for intentionally designing moments that link you together.

Why Bother with Routines?

Establishing routines ensures that you and your tween are interacting and communicating daily. You've noticed that they no longer hang out where you are after school or in the evening as they did in elementary school. Instead, their room is their sanctuary and a safe space where they can feel independent and gain some separation from you, their parent. This individuation is required to become a card-carrying adult. You'll recall that one of your goals is to launch capable, educated, and kind adults. To achieve this, they need time to think, connect with friends, and do nothing. Or maybe do homework or nap or daydream as they become the person they are meant to become.

Their newfound cave doesn't reduce your child to tenant status: they remain an integral member of the family. As such, that closed door is not an actual barrier to you visiting, with or without an agenda. They need you, for you are their parent. And they need to know what to expect and be able to rely on your consistency. They depend on your presence and commitment to them and the family.

The routines you create provide the framework for the interpersonal relationship that is at the core of your lives. From morning greetings to everyone cleaning up together after dinner to singing "Happy Birthday" to the birthday person while they are just waking up and going to church, your message is always that you value them, they are wanted and loved, and they fit and belong.

Creating Your Culture

Children want and need consistent structure. As they grow and change, what remains unchanged and reliable is you and the environment you've created. Your steady leadership, beliefs, and expectations frame their lives and define their center of gravity.

As imperfect humans, both tweens and parents, we have issues that aggravate each other and stifle our best efforts. An example is the tween who can barely drag themself out of bed each morning no matter how much sleep they've had. Or the one who needs to use the bathroom every night during dinner. Or the one who takes your hair dryer and doesn't return it. We know there will always be something that your child will need you to help them through. And they can count on you to be there for them.

And if you're the one who causes discord by losing your temper or being unavailable because you can't put your device down or you're too busy, then it's on you to reflect and see if your actions match your intentions. We can justify that one day won't matter, and it won't, but more than that will.

You've learned that it's up to us to hold it together and build our family's culture so our tweens have experiences that enable them to be successful, solve problems, learn from mistakes, and contribute. Just as your child follows a schedule at school, a similar template is needed at home with defined morning routines all the way through bedtime. Kids gain surety because their day and lives are orderly.

Create Calm with Check-Ins and Clarifications

We create safety and peace by creating calm and not jumping from one crisis to another.

In the story of Eli and the single bag of Oreos, neither Eli nor his mom communicated about the unusual number of bags. A check-in by Mom, or more info from Eli, would have ensured that the seven packages would be ready for the trip to school the next morning. It's easy to think or assume we've communicated well, but until the other person understands exactly what we mean, we have work to do. By the way, I must tell you, I really like it that everyone in the family contributes to the grocery list. That is a cool tool.

We can understand why both Eli and his mom are upset. When I speak publicly about this, I often use a glitter jar to demonstrate how our body responds. Ahead of time, the glass jar is filled with glitter of all sizes and mixed with clear glue. Think of it as a snow globe: if I shake it, all the glitter scatters and flies around, and takes a long time to resettle back to the bottom. This agitating glitter represents the intensity of our emotions with our adrenaline revving up and our hearts beating wildly. The time it takes for the glitter to settle to the bottom of the jar is likely the time it takes for us to feel calm and relaxed once we've been riled.

Equally important in understanding our emotional and physical responses to stress is striving to not let simple things morph into huge conflicts. That way neither you nor your tween have to experience feeling out of control, and then losing time that the mending requires. In the case of the Oreos, Eli could have talked to his mother and explained the science project and why he needed the cookies. And his mom could have contacted him to clarify while she was at the store and saw the number seven in front of the Oreos.

You are busy parents and act on what you know, yet you can expand your point of view by checking in and clarifying.

Expressing Love in Your Child's Love Language

As parents we want to hit the mark, showing our children love in the way that they receive it best. Gary Chapman studied "love languages" and categorized them into five preferences. Following that, he designed a quiz for us to identify ours. If you and your family have not taken the Love Language Quiz, I urge you to. It's like unlocking a secret you didn't know you had. Here's a resource for the quiz: https://www.yourtweenandyou.com/the-love-language-test/.

The five love languages are as follows:

1. **Physical Touch**—This person likes physical expressions such as a pat on the back, hug, fist bump, high five, and other forms of affection.

2. **Words of Affirmation**—This person likes to hear words that affirm and encourage them, such as *I love you*, *I appreciate how hard you work*, *your room looks nice*, *you show real potential for that*, or *I can see you getting better at that every day*.

3. **Receiving Gifts**—This person likes things given to them that are planned out, such as their favorite chips or a new charging cord. It doesn't have to be expensive, and all the things you give them already qualify.

4. **Acts of Service**—This is when someone likes special things done for them, such as bringing in their backpack, matching their socks, or helping them do chores.

5. **Quality Time**—This applies to a person who wants your undivided attention and focus on them, as in doing things together and listening to one another.

> **Once you have each other's quiz results you can plan ways to express your love in their preferred language.**

It makes sense that if your child prefers to be shown love by spending Quality Time together, they'd want to go the store with you or watch something you both enjoy. While affirming them or doing something special for them will be nice and appreciated, it doesn't fill their love bucket. If a child prefers Acts of Service, you can offer to bring them a beverage, find their phone, or match their socks after they do their laundry. If their language is Physical Touch, they will feel loved when you give them a hug, a pat, or a kiss.

What we often do is show love the way we like to receive it because it comes easily to us. But you won't do that. Instead, you will find ways to incorporate your child's love language into your daily actions.

Reinforcing Positive Traits

Look for opportunities throughout the day to describe your child's strengths to them, listing what you see. You can comment on or commend your child's honesty, tenacity, compassion, hard work, planning, organization, loyalty, artistic talent, commitment, sense of justice—whatever wonderfulness you see in them.

I am not advocating constant, mindless praise, for we don't ever want seeking praise to be your child's reason for doing or not doing things. As we talked about in Chapters 4 and 6, you want to empower intrinsic motivation and good character in your child. You know that what matters most is how they see themselves and what they believe to be true about themselves: their perception and self-concept. We can acknowledge their efforts and positive choices with our words.

- "Your sense of style shows in the way you did your hair today."
- "Your plan succeeded when you went to bed early: you got up early and took your shower."
- "You were kind to your sister this morning helping her take her things to the car."
- "You were generous sharing your Halloween candy with your cousin."

From these statements they learn:

- I am artistic
- I am a planner

- I am kind
- I am generous

Because so much is going on in their lives, they don't always process their strengths and abilities. Acknowledging them specifically benefits their **Search for Identity** and gives them language that defines who they are.

Telling them these things is not to make them into a big deal. Rather a casual mention works best. If you're walking past your child's room and you see them putting their laundry away, stop for a moment and say, "You are keeping your room organized." By acknowledging their decision and action, you're reminding them not only that they are organized but also that they have ownership of their choices.

Daily Routines for Parents to Create at Home

There are three times in a day that lend themselves easily to building habits: first thing in the morning, dinnertime, and last thing in the evening. Even if you cannot always make these times work, given realities like school activities or the fact that you are co-parenting, you can establish the expectation that, whenever possible, you and your tween will have designated time together.

Morning Greeting

When you greet your child in the morning, whether it is getting them out of bed or seeing them in the kitchen after they have gotten themselves up, you can make a point to say good morning cheerfully and with a smile. It may seem insignificant, but your greeting lets them know you are glad they are in your life. Plus, a smile gives you joy, too.

If either you or your tween is not a morning person, or if you are not with your tween every morning, the cheery, face-to-face "good morning" may not work. If so, you can try another small ritual. A pat on the arm, handing them a Pop-Tart on their way to the bus, a "good morning" text sent from your home across town, or even opening the door as they leave—all parts of different love languages—are signals that you care about and love them.

Dinnertime

As I've mentioned before, eating dinner together as often as possible is one of the most important routines you can establish for your family. Making it device-free and upbeat makes your kids want to show up for more than the food. You may want to consider these conversation starters: gratitude, reviewing the day and fun, the redo, and what's next. The goal is to make the conversations inclusive while honoring everyone with an open invitation to talk, share, and relax.

Gratitude

Gratitude brings us joy. Even when a day has gone badly, this moment of joy can be a reprieve and even reset our woes. You could state that you were grateful for the open parking space right in front of the orthodontist's office or the sweet text your daughter, who is sitting at the table, sent today. These everyday things make it clear that gratitude isn't just for winning the lottery or scoring the winning goal.

We can't orchestrate gratitude—just like we can't make something good happen. But we can help our children adopt a mindset that promotes gratitude.

Reviewing the Day and Fun

Reviewing the day is not about giving the day a grade. It's letting each person tell their story, have fun together, and feel emotionally supported. Your dinner table is a safe place for everyone to share both wins and disappointments, funny stories, and even learning.

The lighter-hearted and hilarious stories are always welcome, for we want to know that the text that was spelled wrong gave the opposite meaning, and the often grumpy bus driver waited for the student who was usually the first one on the bus and even said hello to her.

A game that is also a learning opportunity is "What would you do if...?" What I like best about it is that the questions can prepare your tween for unforeseen circumstances.

- "What would you do if the teacher called on you and you didn't know the answer?"

- "What would you do if the assistant principal wanted to know something you didn't want to share?"
- "What would you do if you knew your boyfriend/girlfriend were going to break up with you?"
- "What would you do if you lost your phone and needed a ride home?"

The Redo

The redo component invokes the idea of second-tier learning that we discussed in Chapter 7. It's the chance to talk about what we will do differently when faced with a fresh opportunity. This cognitive process supports objective thinking, planning, and problem-solving.

As an example, your child might say, "This Honors History course is too hard and takes up too much of my time. I wish I'd never signed up for it." To which you only say, "Really? It's harder than you expected?" Because you're not trying to change their mind but make them think. They can go on to say, "I know it's too late to change now, but next year I'm not doing it."

What's Next

This is about what's on the agenda, short and long term. Does a child have to hurry through dinner to get to a late play rehearsal tonight? What should we expect at the family reunion next weekend? Can we celebrate a birthday on Tuesday because Wednesday is an away volleyball game? What is the summer vacation shaping up to be?

This feeds into tweens wanting to know what's going on so they can have input and give feedback.

End of Day

Like many other aspects of the tween years, the end-of-day routine will be different from what it used to be, but it will still be a treasured way to keep your relationship strong.

You probably recall the story about Sam, Carrie, and Greg in Chapter 3, and how they collaborated to establish a new end-of-day agreement. Lots of things were decided, including that Greg would "tuck-in" Sam at the end of the day. He saw this time not as reverting to a childhood lullaby but as a chance for them to come together at the end of the day without an agenda.

Whatever you call that moment when you say goodnight to your tween, it is a way to end the day on a positive note. Parents may want to take a few minutes to say what they appreciate about their tween and ask if everything is going okay. When there are no devices, interruptions, or agendas, your child will open their heart, and you can be ready to listen. It can be a very sweet time together.

For other parents and tweens, bedtime is not ideal for a chat or even much of a conversation—or the realities of your schedule may prevent you from being physically present. You can instead find a way to bookend the day that works for them and still make it an opportunity for connection. You may stand in the doorway and say a quick "Sleep tight, I love you," or "See you in the morning!" You may give your tween a wordless wink and a pat on the head. You may text "Good night" earlier if you are co-parenting and your child is with their other parent.

The end-of-day moment comes down to being a presence for our child before they sleep. Like the "good morning" moment, it's a chance to show our tween we are there for them, always.

The Day in Action: Eli's Story

These practices increase your engagement with each other and decrease crises that interrupt flow. Let's see what could have helped Eli and his parents avoid the Oreo showdown.

At dinner on Thursday, when Roger asks everyone what's next for them, Eli says, "I told the teacher I'd bring in Oreos for a science lab on Monday. Is that okay?" He takes a big bite of pasta.

"Sure," says Rachel. "How many do you need?"

Eli mumbles something through his mouthful. "Oops. Sorry." He swallows and tries again. "Seven packages of regular Oreos. That'll be enough for everyone in class."

"Okay," Rachel nods. "Put it on the grocery list—but make a note next to it so I remember why I'm getting hundreds of cookies." She returns to wiping Willa's face, and the conversation moves on.

Unfortunately, when Eli uses the grocery list app, he forgets to add that note, and when his mom is at the store on Sunday, she thinks the number is a mistake and only buys one package of Oreos.

At dinnertime that evening, when Roger asks what's next, Eli says, "I'm excited about getting to do that cookie lab tomorrow. Thanks for supplying the Oreos."

Rachel's stomach sinks. "Oh no," she says. "I only bought one package of cookies! I'm so sorry."

Eli frowns. "But everyone's counting on me!"

"Did you remember to put a note on the list?" Roger asks. He picks up some peas Willa has flung onto the table.

Eli sighs. "No."

"It's okay," Roger says. "One of us will go to the store after dinner."

"In fact," Rachel adds, knowing that Eli's love language is Quality Time, "why don't you and I go together, Eli?"

The late errand turns out to be a bonus, as the two of them joke about all the shoppers having less than three things in their carts and how no one remembered a reusable bag, including them. And Eli's ears perk up when he hears his favorite question: "Is there anything else you'd like?"

That night, when Rachel says good night, she stands in Eli's doorway and says, "I had fun with you at the grocery store, Eli. I'm kind of glad we had the mix-up."

Eli smiles. "Yeah, but next time, I'll remember to put that note on the list."

It's a small moment but added in with the hundreds of other moments where you've shown that you love, respect, and care about your child.

Key Takeaways

By creating daily routines for their children, parents can make their relationship with their tweens extraordinary. It may seem like tweens are all about separation, but they need a strong connection with us, and routines make their bumpy days a little smoother. Small habits like morning greetings, dinnertime conversations, and bedtime check-ins can have big results—they can help us avoid crises, show tweens love, and help them with their identity and sense of belonging.

Our role as parents is to create boundaries, not just the walls of our house but the structure and habits of the day. Tweens count on the stability of routines and moments of connection that assure them, *My parent really cares about me. They accept me, trust me, and respect me.*

Your Key Takeaways: Your Turn to Write

Name three things you learned.

1. _____

2. _____

3. _____

Name two awarenesses you'll embrace.

1. _____

2. _____

Name at least one thing you will apply. What will you do differently?

1. _____

Conclusion

Y ou are not the same person you were when you picked up this book. Now you're well acquainted with the **Trio of Trials:** **Puberty**, the **Search for Identity**, and the **Immature Prefrontal Cortex**. You recognize the influence and power these trials have on your tween, and that your purpose is to prepare them for successful adulthood. You've reinvented your parenting style, letting go of the authoritarian style needed for younger children, and accepted an authoritative role because it cultivates trust and relationship-building. It has not been easy adjusting to your changing child or your new role; fortunately, you are fully equipped and confident leading your child.

Your Leadership

You've honed fresh leadership skills that empower you to approach your child with mindful compassion, curiosity, and empathy. Because your role is guiding and coaching, rather than managing, you've shifted the ownership of your child's tasks to them, given them a voice to be heard, and fostered their personal accountability. Your insight makes it possible for your child to gradually gain the autonomy and independence they badly desire and need. You've learned to see situations from their perspective, actively listen before responding, and regulate your emotions. You value understanding your child first, and only then giving feedback or influencing them. And you love knowing that by asking open-ended questions, you eliminate receiving the dreaded one-word answers.

Your Shared Journey

You've embraced how incredibly wonderful and, at the same time, horribly frustrating these years can be for your tween. And, at times, for you, too. You've implemented habits and routines for the ordinary moments of everyday life. You don't rely on grand gestures to express your love or gain favor. You've become wiser on this shared journey, knowing that showing up, being present and available, means ever so much more to your child than they can comprehend. Your goal is to parent intentionally in order to launch a well-educated, responsible, and kind contributor to society.

Your Humanity

You have overcome the tendency to blame your child for all that is not going well during this stage of development. You've learned how to apologize with vulnerability and humility—and to accept apologies with grace and forgiveness. You've updated your understanding of mental health to include the reality that the need for it is as paramount as physical health. Your comfort level and confidence chatting with your child about sex, reproduction, gender roles, and consent has increased. You've crafted a mindset to collaborate with your child to solve problems together, avoid punitive measures, and transform mistakes into learning and resilience-building opportunities.

Your Progress

As your better angles and intentions influence your parenting paradigm, you acknowledge that the fruits of change are accompanied by your consistency and patience. You like to see and measure growth, but for us humans, it's neither instant nor linear: you know there will be bumps and hurdles along the path for both you and your tween. If your child is co-parented, the skills and tools you've added to your parenting playbook are not dependent on the other parent doing the same thing. You know that each human has their own distinct relationship with others. You're grateful you are in the world of progress with your child, not the world of perfection. Please give yourself a pat on the back for taking this higher road raising your beloved child.

Your Future

While the future isn't written, it's refreshing and reassuring to know that your relationship with your child is what you make it to be every day. You are not alone on this journey, for the parents of your child's friends share the same path. You'll find their kindness and support to be immensely helpful. You can subscribe to receive *The Tween Times*, a newsletter with tips and support for parents of tweens that will pop up in your inbox (https://www.yourtweenandyou.com/blog). In addition, for personal support, you can reach out to me and my team for parent coaching to augment what you've learned.

I have full confidence in you and the extraordinary child you love.

Acknowledgments

It's from the deepest part of the largest ocean and my heart that my gratitude extends to my family, friends, readers, coaches, parents of tweens, educators, mentors, and editors who believed in me and my mission. When I waned, wavered, and celebrated, you stood by me with generous empathy, encouragement, and applause. A million thanks for being you.

About the Author

JoAnn Schauf founded Your Tween and You, writes her blog, *The Tween Times*, coaches parents and adolescents, and speaks at conferences and to parent groups. After earning her master of science in counseling, she worked as a therapist in a psychiatric hospital and served as a counselor in secondary schools and colleges. Her interactions with parents of tweens who were confounded by their children's responses to adolescence coupled with technology's interference led her to write *Loving the Alien: How to Parent a Tween.* As the parent of four, she experienced the same challenges and frustrations! JoAnn calls Austin, Texas, home and spends her free time with family, volunteering, and on the beach in California.

You can reach her at https://www.yourtweenandyou.com/get-in-touch/.

www.ingramcontent.com/pod-product-compliance
Lightning Source LLC
Chambersburg PA
CBHW042315120626
46547CB00022B/2092